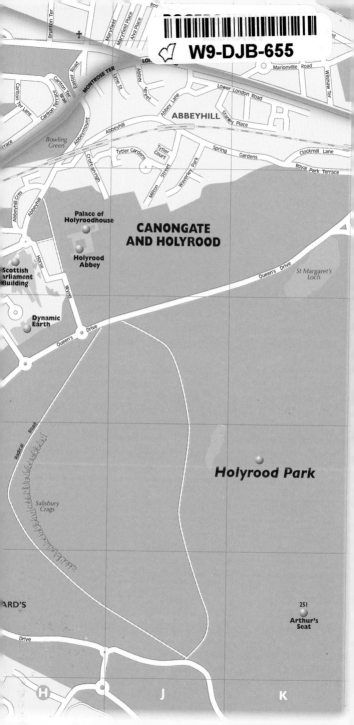

CANONGATE AND HOLYROOD

ABBEYHILL

Marionville Road

Lower London Road

Stanley Place

Spring Gardens

Clockmill Lane

Royal Park Terrace

Bowling Green

Tytler Gardens

Tytler Court

Milton Street

Waverley Park

Palace of Holyroodhouse

Holyrood Abbey

Scottish Parliament Building

Dynamic Earth

Queen's Drive

St Margaret's Loch

Queen's Drive

Radical Road

Salisbury Crags

Holyrood Park

251 Arthur's Seat

ARD'S

Drive

MONTROSE TER

Brunton Ter

Easter Road

Carlton Ter Lane

Carlton Ter

Carlton Ter Brae

Abbeymount

Abbeyhill

Abbeyhill Cres

Abbeyhill

Horse Wynd

Wynd

Maryfield

Maryfield Place

Alva Place

Abbey Lane

Abbey Street

Lime St

Wishaw Ter

H J K

Fodor's
25 Best

EDINBURGH

How to Use This Book

This guide is divided into four sections

● Essential Edinburgh: An introduction to the city and tips on making the most of your stay.

● Edinburgh by Area: We've broken the city into four areas, and recommended the best sights, shops, entertainment venues, nightlife and places to eat in each one. Suggested walks help you to explore on foot.

● Where to Stay: The best hotels, whether you're looking for luxury, budget or something in between.

● Need to Know: The info you need to make your trip run smoothly, including getting about by public transportation, weather tips, emergency phone numbers and useful websites.

Navigation In the Edinburgh by Area chapter, we've given each area its own color, which is also used on the locator maps throughout the book and the map on the inside front cover.

Maps The fold-out map with this book is a comprehensive street plan of Edinburgh. The grid on this fold-out map is the same as the grid on the locator maps within the book. We've given grid references within the book for each sight and listing.

Contents

Introducing Edinburgh

Edinburgh, Scotland's appealing capital city, attracts many thousands of visitors every year. They come for many reasons: to seek their ancestral roots, to experience the Festival or just to get a taste of what makes Scotland tick.

Few first-time visitors are prepared for the sheer majesty of the city and the richness of its history and culture. Edinburgh combines its past with all that's best in 21st-century life, making it a popular destination and a jumping-off point for exploring Scotland.

Reminders of the past are everywhere. The castle rises over the tall tenements, narrow streets and dark *vennels* (alleyways) of the Old Town while, to the north, the broad streets and spacious squares of the New Town are lined with gracious 18th-century buildings. Look closer, though, and it becomes clear that the city is much more than a tourist hub existing as a living museum or theme park of the Enlightenment.

Scottish monarchs lived in Edinburgh as early as the 11th century, but the city did not become the royal capital until the reign of King James II (*r.* 1437–60). Political power moved to London with the Act of Union in 1707, but the Scotland Act of 1998 created a devolved Scottish Parliament, sitting in a dramatic building at Holyrood. The economy is dominated by the service sector, with the emphasis on financial services, which has encouraged growing numbers of young, ambitious, highly paid professionals. It's these people, rather than the visitors, who have charged the city's renaissance, turning the capital into a slick and stylish metropolis, whose quality of life is rated among the highest in the world.

Take time to participate in some of the pleasures enjoyed by local people—plays, music, bar-hopping and the club scene—rather than a steady diet of tartan-obsessed Caledonian entertainment.

FACTS AND FIGURES

- The population of Edinburgh is around half a million. This swells to more than one million during the Festival in August.
- Together, Edinburgh's Old Town and New Town contain more than 4,500 listed buildings.
- The highest point is Arthur's Seat.
- The Water of Leith is the city's longest waterway at 35km (22 miles).

FIRE, FIRE

Edinburgh was one of the world's first cities to have a municipal fire service. It was founded in 1824 by local man James Braidwood (1800–61), who was recognized for his heroism in tackling raging fires of that year in High Street. He later moved to London, forming the precursor to the London Fire Brigade, but was killed in the Tooley Street fire.

FESTIVAL TIME

Edinburgh's Festival is not one event but many, running concurrently in August. The most prestigious is the Edinburgh International Festival, founded in 1947, which showcases world-class performing arts events. Side by side with this heavyweight, the anarchic and vast Fringe has plays, music, comedy and dance in more than 300 venues.

MILITARY TATTOO

Book early for this one. The spectacle, held on the castle Esplanade with military precision—the swirl of the kilts, the skirling of the pipes—is the greatest tattoo of them all (tickets: ☎ 0131 225 1188; edintattoo.co.uk). It takes place Monday–Saturday evenings for three weeks in August. At other times of the year, get an insight at the visitor center.

A Short Stay in Edinburgh

DAY 1

Morning Most popular is a stroll down the **Royal Mile** (▷ 28–29). Those who don't want to walk can take the **hop-on-hop-off bus** (▷ 119) to visit the major sights. Get to **Edinburgh Castle** (▷ 24–25) at opening time to avoid the crowds. Close by is the **Camera Obscura** (▷ 32). Take a bit of time to explore the alleyways (*vennels* and *wynds*) as you walk away from the castle along Castlehill.

Mid-morning Divert right to explore Victoria Street, with its specialist shops. If you want to walk farther, continue onto West Bow and out into the attractive **Grassmarket** (▷ 32–33), with lots of opportunities for coffee. Retrace your steps and continue along the Royal Mile into Lawnmarket and along to High Street. Take a look at **St. Giles' Cathedral** (▷ 30).

Lunch Have lunch at **The Mitre** (▷ 43), diagonally opposite the Tron.

Afternoon Continue on High Street, where you will find the **Museum of Childhood** (▷ 54) and **John Knox House** (▷ 60) opposite. Continue onto Canongate, with the **Museum of Edinburgh** (▷ 55) on the right and **Canongate Tolbooth** (▷ 50–51) on the left. As you near the end of the road you will see the dramatic **Scottish Parliament Building** (▷ 58–59) on the right and shortly afterward, the **Palace of Holyroodhouse** (▷ 56–57).

Dinner For old-fashioned charm at a price try the **Witchery by the Castle** (▷ 44). For a taste of France, head for **Petit Paris** (▷ 44).

Evening Just to the west of the Old Town you will find **Usher Hall** (▷ 41), where you can take in a classical concert. If clubbing is more your thing, try **Cabaret Voltaire** (▷ 40).

DAY 2

Morning Start at the Waverley Station end of **Princes Street** (▷ 74). You can then decide if you want to explore the shops along the famous road or those behind it. Those preferring art can visit the **Scottish National Gallery** (▷ 72–73), just beyond the **Scott Monument** (▷ 76). It is possible to take the free link bus from here to the other galleries.

Mid-morning Have a coffee at the gallery or try **VinCaffè** (▷ 86), an Italian bar and restaurant inside **Jenners** (▷ 79) on Princes Street. You can then explore the maze-like department store for a spot of retail therapy.

Lunch Take a pub lunch on Rose Street, which once boasted the most pubs of any street in Edinburgh. The **Mussel Inn** (▷ 86) is a good choice for seafood lovers.

Afternoon Catch a bus from Princes Street out to **Leith** (▷ 92–93) and visit the **Royal Yacht *Britannia*** (▷ 95) and the Ocean Terminal Centre if you fancy a bit of shopping. Take a walk along The Shore, with its trendy bars and smart restaurants.

Dinner Back in New Town, eat on the popular George Street. Try the Italian **Contini** (▷ 83) or, for smart dining, the **Dome** (▷ 84).

Evening Still on George Street, try the most fashionable clubs **Lulu** (▷ 82) or **Shanghai** (▷ 83) in the boutique hotels Tigerlily and Le Monde. Alternatively, the Omni Centre at Greenside Place on Leith Street has a luxurious multiscreen cinema, while the **Edinburgh Playhouse** (▷ 81) next door, a former cinema and now a multipurpose auditorium, puts on musicals, dance and rock concerts.

▶ ▶ ▶

Arthur's Seat ▷ 48–49
Looming above Edinburgh, this extinct volcano offers fantastic views of the city.

Calton Hill ▷ 68 This hill in the city center is crowned by a collection of historic monuments.

Canongate Tolbooth ▷ 50–51 This attractive building houses a museum of everyday life.

Scottish Parliament Building ▷ 58–59 Controversial, expensive, but certainly striking, this building opened in 2004.

Scottish National Gallery of Modern Art ▷ 98 The place to view 20th-century Scottish art and sculpture.

Scottish National Gallery ▷ 72–73 A breathtaking collection of artistic masterpieces.

Scotch Whisky Experience ▷ 31 Your chance to learn more about Scotland's national drink and to taste a wee dram.

St. Giles' Cathedral ▷ 30 This imposing church, dedicated to Edinburgh's patron saint, became a cathedral in the 17th century.

RZSS Edinburgh Zoo ▷ 96–97 A conscientious approach to animals and their conservation.

Royal Yacht *Britannia* ▷ 95 All aboard the most regal of ships—a must for royal buffs.

Royal Mile ▷ 28–29 The straight road all the way from Edinburgh Castle to the Palace of Holyroodhouse.

Royal Botanic Garden ▷ 94 A green oasis in a busy capital—there's year-round interest here.

Royal Botanic Garden

STOCKBRIDGE

BROUGHTON

NEW TOWN
65–86

Queen Street Gardens

Georgian House

NEW TOWN

Scottish National Gallery

RZSS Edinburgh Zoo, Scottish National Gallery of Modern Art

Princes Street and Gardens

Royal Mile

Muse Chil

St Giles' Cathedral

Edinburgh Castle

Scotch Whisky Experience

OLD TOWN
20–44

Greyfriars Kirk

Natio Museu Scotla

OLD TOWN

SOUTH SIDE

Meadow Park

Bruntsfield Links

These pages are a quick guide to the Top 25, which are described in more detail later. Here they are listed alphabetically, and the tinted background shows which area they are in.

Craigmillar Castle
▷ **90–91** A trip out to this castle makes a pleasant change from city bustle.

Dynamic Earth ▷ **52** Fun science with great effects and interactive enjoyment.

Edinburgh Castle
▷ **24–25** A million visitors a year come to Scotland's most famous castle.

Georgian House ▷ **69** Take a tour for a taste of 18th-century New Town elegance.

Greyfriars Kirk ▷ **26** Many elaborate memorials, including the most famous of all, Greyfriars Bobby.

Holyrood Park ▷ **53** Take a walk on the wild side in this craggy park.

Leith ▷ **92–93** Edinburgh's seaport and now a trendy tourist area.

Museum of Childhood
▷ **54** Nostalgia and fun abound in this museum for big and little kids.

Museum of Edinburgh
▷ **55** A treasure house of information and objects all about Edinburgh.

National Museum of Scotland ▷ **27** A hugely entertaining introduction to Scottish history and culture.

Princes Street and Gardens ▷ **74** After shopping in this famous street, relax in the gardens.

Palace of Holyroodhouse
▷ **56–57** A royal palace rich with historical associations and works of art.

New Town ▷ **70–71** 18th-century planning at its best—a prime example of Georgian architecture.

Map labels:
Leith, Royal Yacht *Britannia*
Quarryhole Park
Eastern Cemetery
LOCHEND
HILLSIDE
NORTON PARK
Lochend Park
SIDE
MEADOWBANK
CANONGATE AND HOLYROOD 45-64
Palace of Holyroodhouse
gate
Scottish Parliament Building
Dynamic Earth
m of rgh
Salisbury Crags
Holyrood Park
St Margaret's Loch
Dunsapie Loch
LEONARD'S
251
Arthur's Seat
gmillar Castle
Duddingston Loch

◀ ◀ ◀

Shopping

Edinburgh attracts shoppers from all over the world, some looking for designer styles, others hunting authentically Scottish antiques, arts and crafts, cashmere and tartan or fine whiskies.

Get Off the Beaten Track

If quirky independent stores are your thing, seek out vintage stores, small galleries and idiosyncratic design boutiques on the medieval Grassmarket. Other rich hunting grounds are provided by villagey Stockbridge, fashionable Broughton Street or William Street in the West End. Edinburgh's main museums and galleries sell books, ceramics, jewelry, textiles and prints inspired by their collections. Fans of sword and sorcery epics and movies like *Braveheart* and *Rob Roy* will find accurate replicas of Highland dirks and broadswords alongside fantasy weaponry in several specialist stores in the Old Town.

Edinburgh has always been a literary city, so bibliophiles will find a better-than-average selection of antiquarian and independent bookshops specializing in everything from art and Scottish history to fantasy and science fiction. Wizarding fans should make tracks for the Harry Potter store at 40 Victoria Street, which inspired J.K. Rowling's Diagon Alley.

Made in Scotland

If you're looking for something typically Scottish, you'll be spoiled for choice whatever your budget. Tartans, tweeds and cashmeres are

---

MARKETS

Sunday sees thousands of locals heading out to Ingliston, which is home to a huge, inexpensive and vibrant outdoor market with more than 100 stands and a rummage sale thrown in. Undercover markets include the rambling New Street Sunday Market in Old Town. For the best in Scottish produce, the Saturday Farmers' Market (9–2), held on Castle Terrace, is worth a trawl for superb organic meat, vegetables and other foods (edinburghfarmersmarket.co.uk).

From traditional to wacky, designer to vintage—Edinbur has it all

everywhere, and smaller stores sell designer knitted goods in rainbow hues, or tartan with a twist, bringing Scottish style right up to date. Tartan can be found in the form of everything from a blanket to a kilt. Local craftspeople are celebrated for their silver, metalwork and jewelry, and you'll find samples at the top city stores or among dozens of tiny studio-workshops. You can find the country's musical heritage in a huge range of CDs—everything from reels and pipe-and-drum music to Celtic rock and traditional Gaelic song. Books, posters and calendars make great gifts, and you'll find an excellent selection here. Edinburgh is also well endowed with expensive antiques shops and fine art and contemporary galleries. Urban sophisticates can bypass all this to focus on fur-niture and objets d'art that combine traditional craftsmanship with cutting-edge design, not just from Scotland but from all over the world.

A Taste of Scotland

Food is always a popular souvenir, and shops sell the best of the country's produce, often vacuum-packed to make transportation easier. Choose from wild smoked salmon, Orkney cheese, heather honey and soft fruit jam, short-bread, oatcakes, and a bottle of the finest malt whisky from the huge range you'll find, some of which are 100 years old. Just remember to check your country's rules on food imports.

SHOPPING AREAS

The city's retail heart beats in Princes Street, and if you're looking for chain stores it's the best choice; if not, with the exception of the excellent department store Jenners, it can be avoided. For souvenirs, head for the Old Town, where tartan, tat, sweaters and whisky crowd the shelves. The New Town's best shops are around Queen Street, with big-name, classy shopping at Multrees Walk (▷ 79) off St. Andrew's Square—home to the beautiful Harvey Nichols. For good local shops, head for Stockbridge, Bruntsfield and Morningside. For style, William Street, in the city's West End, has some great specialist shops.

Shopping by Theme

Whether you're looking for a department store, a quirky boutique, or something in between, you'll find it all in Edinburgh. On this page shops are listed by theme. For a more detailed write-up, see the individual listings in Edinburgh by Area.

Edinburgh by Night

In summer the city fairly buzzes with all the activities of the festivals and their fringes, catering for every taste and budget. However, there's plenty to do at any time of the year.

Music, Theater, Dance and Film
Outside the Festival, Edinburgh has a year-round schedule of the performing arts, with plays, music, opera, dance, ballet, comedy, folk music, rock and jazz all on offer, while cinemas show blockbusters and art-house movies. You can find listings information in *The List* (list.co.uk), a magazine that details every type of entertainment. Tickets for major performances can be booked through Ticketmaster (ticketmaster.co.uk), in the VisitScotland office (3 Princes Street, Mon–Sat 9–5, Sun 10–5; till 6 or 7 in the summer) or at venues.

Calmer Pleasures
If you're looking for a quieter evening, the city looks fantastic after dark, with many landmark buildings illuminated. Except for the Festival weeks, restaurants in Edinburgh tend to wind down around 10pm (though some smaller eateries stay open much later); eat around 8pm, then head for a stylish bar or traditional pub.

Dance the Night Away
Edinburgh's clubs are far more subdued than those of Glasgow, London or Manchester and, as in many other cities, are often in a state of flux, with venues and clubs changing from one month to the next. Friday and Saturday are the big nights, when admission prices rise and places stay open later. Check out *The List* or the free sheet *Metro,* available Monday to Saturday.

inburgh offers a full range of tions for a night out, includtheater, pubs, dance and ditional celebrations

HOGMANAY
Hogmanay is Scotland's New Year, and Edinburgh celebrates it in style with a four-day spectacle that includes concerts, street parties, live music, marching bands, processions and spectacular fireworks. Tickets go on sale in July from edinburghshogmanay.com.

Where to Eat

The culinary explorer is spoiled for choice in cosmopolitan Edinburgh. You don't have to look hard for traditional Scottish cuisine, but there are plenty of alternatives to be found, from Thai and Indian to Turkish and Moroccan.

Where and When to Eat

Restaurants reflect the diversity of British culture and there are options to suit most tastes and pockets. Some of the city's more formal restaurants are open only for lunch and dinner, but you can find somewhere to eat in Edinburgh from as early as 9am until midnight and even later. Many city center pubs serve unpretentious, decent meals all day. Many top restaurants are based in hotels, but you don't need to be staying at the hotel to enjoy the cuisine, although it is best to book in advance. Traditional tea shops are excellent for snacks and are usually open from mid-morning until 4 or 5pm. There are some good options in the larger department stores for light lunches and tea and coffee breaks.

International Dining

Ambitious, innovative cooking based on locally sourced produce and traditional recipes is easy to find, but Edinburgh also offers a good range of international restaurants, including long-established Italian trattorias. With the influx of Italian immigrants to Scotland in the early 20th century, you will find good pasta and, of course, the quintessential Italian-made ice cream.

Scotland's fresh produce can often be sampled outside as well as indoors

SCOTTISH SELECTION

Arbroath smokies—small hot-smoked haddock.
clootie dumpling—steamed sweet-and-spicy pudding, traditionally cooked in a cloth.
cranachan—raspberries, cream and toasted oatmeal.
crowdie—light curd cheese.
Cullen skink—creamy fish broth based on "Finnan haddie," or smoked haddock.
Forfar bridie—pasty made with beef, onion and potato.

Where to Eat by Cuisine

There are plenty of places to eat to suit all tastes and budgets in Edinburgh. On this page they are listed by cuisine. For a more detailed description of each restaurant, see Edinburgh by Area.

Asian
Chop Chop (▷ 106)
Educated Flea (▷ 84)
Kweilin (▷ 85)

Bistros
Bell's Diner (▷ 83)
The Canons' Gait (▷ 64)
Dome (▷ 84)
Eden's Kitchen (▷ 84)
Magnum (▷ 85)
Olive Branch (▷ 86)
Smoke Stack (▷ 86)
Voodoo Rooms (▷ 86)
Whiski Rooms (▷ 44)

Fine Dining
Restaurant Martin Wishart (▷ 106)
Rhubarb (▷ 106)

Fish/Seafood
Fishers Leith (▷ 106)
Mussel Inn (▷ 85)
Ondine (▷ 43)
The Ship on the Shore (▷ 106)
Teuchters Landing (▷ 106)

French
Le Café St. Honoré (▷ 83)
La Garrigue (▷ 85)
Petit Paris (▷ 44)
La P'tite Folie (▷ 86)

Italian
Contini Ristorante (▷ 83)
Vincaffè (▷ 86)

Mexican
Miro's (▷ 85)

Mideastern
Hanam's (▷ 43)

Scottish Cuisine
Amber Restaurant (▷ 42)
Angels with Bagpipes (▷ 42)
Deacon Brodie's Tavern (▷ 42)
Dubh Prais Restaurant (▷ 64)
Gallery Restaurant at the Guildford Arms (▷ 84)
Grain Store (▷ 43)

Howies (▷ 85)
The Mitre (▷ 43)
One Square (▷ 44)
Tower Restaurant (▷ 44)
Witchery by the Castle (▷ 44)

Snacks/Light Bites
Bennets Bar (▷ 42)
Coro the Chocolate Café (▷ 84)
Elephant House (▷ 42)
Innis & Gunn Brewery Taproom (▷ 43)
MUMS (▷ 43)
Starbank Inn (▷ 106)

Vegetarian/Vegan
David Bann (▷ 64)
Henderson's Vegan Restaurant (▷ 85)
Holy Cow (▷ 85)
Novapizza (▷ 86)

Top Tips For…

These great suggestions will help you tailor your ideal visit to Edinburgh, no matter how you choose to spend your time. Each suggestion has a fuller write-up elsewhere in the book.

SCOTTISH SOUVENIRS

Kilts and all things tartan can be found at Geoffrey (Tailor) Kiltmakers (▷ 62) and their Tartan Weaving Mill, right by the castle.

Scottish shortbread and fudge are sold at Cranachan & Crowdie (▷ 62).

Try a wee dram—there's a huge choice of Scotland's national tipple at Royal Mile Whiskies (▷ 39).

See the work of local craftspeople at Just Scottish (▷ 39).

Jane Davidson (▷ 79) offers exclusive cashmere from top designers.

For the very best quality, shop at Hawico (▷ 38), but it comes at a price.

SCOTTISH FOOD

Enjoy top dining and Scottish classics with a contemporary twist at the Witchery (▷ 44).

Sample top Scottish cuisine at Dubh Prais Restaurant (▷ 64), with everything from haggis to venison and salmon.

Try the Whiski Rooms (▷ 44) near the Royal Mile for hundreds of malt whiskies and a menu that emphasizes locally produced meat, game and seafood.

Dine amid Victorian splendor at the Gallery Restaurant at the Guildford Arms (▷ 84).

VEGAN AND VEGETARIAN DINING

Head for David Bann (▷ 64) for modern takes on classic vegan and vegetarian dishes.

Holy Cow (▷ 85) in New Town is a wholly vegan café with a fun vibe and a good selection of hot and cold options.

Try Hendersons Vegan restaurant (▷ 85), which, in its various guises, has been providing meat-free meals to Edinburghers for over 50 years.

Clockwise from top left: superior malt whisky makes a great gift; eating outside a Petit Paris; Arthur's Seat;

INTERNATIONAL COOKING

Home-loving Italian is the dish of the day at Contini (▷ 83).

Enjoy French cuisine in a delightful country-style bistro in the heart of the city at Petit Paris (▷ 44).

Dine on fresh seafood at the Mussel Inn (▷ 86), simply prepared and a delight to the taste buds.

A taste of Mexico can be found at Miro's (▷ 85) in New Town's Rose Street.

A BREATH OF FRESH AIR

Classical Edinburgh can be found at the top of Calton Hill (▷ 68).

For some salty air head out to Leith (▷ 92–93) and go aboard the Royal Yacht *Britannia* (▷ 95).

In the heart of the city stroll in the delightful Princes Street Gardens (▷ 74).

If you are feeling energetic get down to Holyrood Park (▷ 53) and climb up to Arthur's Seat (▷ 48–49).

BOUTIQUE HOTELS

Stay in a historic New Town building in glamorous 12 Picardy Place (▷ 110), superbly located just off York Place.

Enjoy spectacular views of Calton Hill from the comfort of your bedroom at the Glasshouse (▷ 112).

One of the coolest hotels in town is The Bonham (▷ 112), nicely located in the West End.

Georgian elegance and sophistication can be found at The Raeburn (▷ 111).

EXPLORING ON FOOT

The best way to get to know the city is to wander its streets and investigate its hidden corners—try one of the self-guided walks in this book (▷ 36, 61, 77).

Join a themed guided walk (▷ 119) to explore a particular aspect of the city, for example haunted Edinburgh, or underground.

...urant in The Bonham
...; Glasshouse hotel;
...dersons Vegan restaurant;
...rsoft Scottish cashmere

SAVING MONEY

Buy day tickets for 24 hours of unlimited central zone bus and tram travel (▷ 118).

Try the all-you-can-eat Chinese banquet at Chop Chop (▷ 106).

The National Museum of Scotland (▷ 27) and the Scottish National Gallery (▷ 72–73) are both free and packed with treasures.

Picnic in the park at Princes Street Gardens (▷ 74) in the city center or the Royal Botanic Garden (▷ 94).

A KID'S DAY OUT

See the animals at the world-renowned zoo (▷ 96–97).

Give yourself a scare in The Edinburgh Dungeon (▷ 75).

Be hands-on and scientific at the terrific Dynamic Earth (▷ 52).

It's free at the Museum of Childhood (▷ 54).

GETTING ACTIVE

Play a round of golf just outside the city (▷ 105, panel).

Enjoy a swim at the Royal Commonwealth Pool (▷ 105).

See Scottish football at Hearts or Hibs (▷ 105).

Spend a day at the races—check out the horses at Musselburgh Racecourse (▷ 105).

GOING OUT ON THE TOWN

Traditional music can be found at Sandy Bells Bar (▷ 40, panel).

Go clubbing at Lulu (▷ 82), in the trendy Tigerlily hotel.

Groove all night at Cabaret Voltaire (▷ 40).

Some great jazz, soul and blues bands appear at The Jazz Bar (▷ 40).

GOING OUT OF THE TOWN

Step back into Edinburgh's tempestuous past at Craigmillar Castle (▷ 90).

Delve into a world of secrets and mystery at Rosslyn Chapel (▷ 102).

From top: Scottish National Gallery; the zoo; grisly fright at the Edinburgh Dungeon; take to the dance floor

Edinburgh by Area

Old Town

The essence of old Edinburgh can be found in this district, with its narrow alleys, ancient *wynds* and compact lanes. The Old Town sees the start of the Royal Mile, dominated by the impressive castle.

Top 25

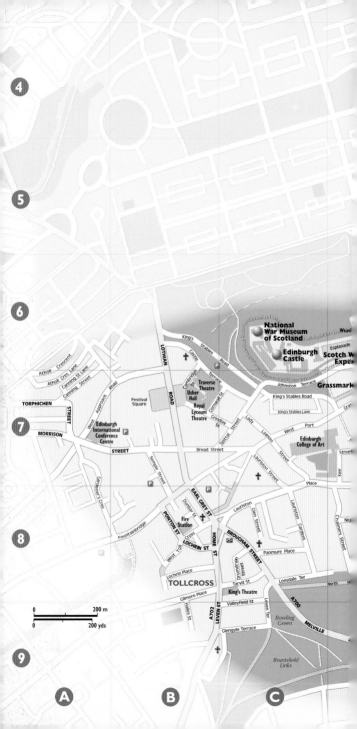

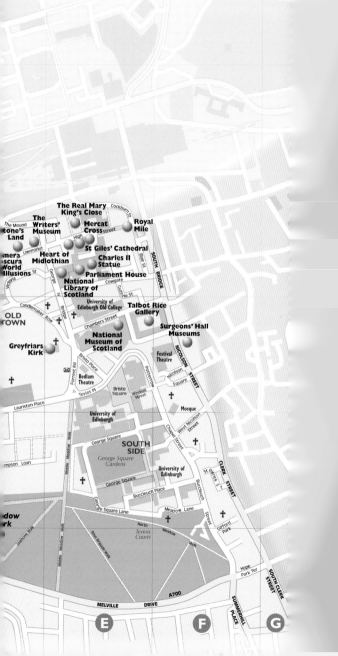

The Real Mary
King's Close

Cockburn Street

The Writers'
Museum

The Mound

tone's
Land

Mercat
Cross

High Street

Royal
Mile

mera
scura
World
Illusions

Victoria St

Heart of
Midlothian

St Giles' Cathedral

Charles II
Statue

Blair St

SOUTH BRIDGE

Parliament House

Cowgate

George IV Bridge

Candlemaker Row

National
Library of
Scotland

Guthrie St

University of
Edinburgh Old College

Talbot Rice
Gallery

OLD
TOWN

Chambers Street

Surgeons' Hall
Museums

Greyfriars
Kirk

National
Museum of
Scotland

Forrest Rd

Bristo Place

NICOLSON STREET

Festival
Theatre

Bedlam
Theatre

Teviot Pl

Bristo
Square

Potterrow

Nicolson
Square

Windmill
Street

Lauriston Place

University of
Edinburgh

West Nicolson
Street

Mosque

mpson Loan

Middle Meadow Walk

George Square

SOUTH
SIDE

George Square
Gardens

Chapel Street

University of
Edinburgh

CLERK STREET

St Patrick St

George Square

Buccleuch Place

Buccleuch Street

dow
rk

George Square Lane

Meadow Lane

North
Tennis
Courts

Middle Meadow Walk

Boroughloch Walk

Melbourne

Gifford Park

Jawbone Walk

Hope
Park Ter

SOUTH CLERK STREET

A700

MELVILLE DRIVE

SUMMERHILL PLACE

E   **F**   **G**

Edinburgh Castle

HIGHLIGHTS

- Great views
- St. Margaret's Chapel
- Mons Meg
- Prisons of War Exhibition
- Scottish Crown Jewels
- Stone of Destiny
- One O'Clock Gun

TIP

- The nearest car parking zones are at Castle Terrace and Johnston Terrace. Visitors with disabilities can park at the castle (reserve ahead ☎ 0131 310 5114).

Perched high on a wedge of volcanic rock, the castle is a symbol of the Scottish nation, reflecting 1,000 years of history in a mix of architectural styles.

Might and majesty As you wind your way up the Castle Rock you can enjoy the view north over the city. The cannons along the battery were a picturesque improvement suggested by Queen Victoria, while the One O'Clock Gun, a field gun from World War II, fires from Mills Mount Battery at precisely 1pm. To enter the castle, you first cross the Esplanade, the setting for the annual Military Tattoo (▷ 5).

Once inside The oldest structure in the castle is the 12th-century chapel, dedicated to St. Margaret by her son, David I. The chapel is

Clockwise from far left: Full military pageant at the annual Edinburgh Tattoo, staged at the castle; stained-glass window depicting Queen Margaret inside St. Margaret's Chapel; the proud fortress overlooks the city; St. Margaret's Chapel; bands at the Tattoo; Mons Meg cannon on the ramparts

almost overshadowed by the huge cannon on the rampart outside—Mons Meg, a gift in 1457 to James II from the Duke of Burgundy, who wished to support the Scots against the English.

Castle of contrasts Be prepared for crowds in the Crown Room, where the Scottish Crown Jewels and the Stone of Destiny are displayed. The crown, dating from 1540, is made of Scottish gold, studded with semiprecious stones from the Cairngorms. The sword and scepter were papal gifts. Scottish kings were crowned on the Stone of Destiny—taken by Edward I, it was recovered from London's Westminster Abbey in 1996. The castle also contains the National War Museum of Scotland (▷ 34), the Scottish National War Memorial and the Prisons of War Exhibition.

THE BASICS

edinburghcastle.scot

✚ C6

✉ Castlehill EH1 2NG

☎ 0131 225 9846

🕐 Apr–Sep daily 9.30–6; Oct–Mar daily 9.30–5; last entry 1 hr beforehand

🍴 Cafés

🚌 23, 27, 41, 42, 67

♿ Some areas are restricted; call first. A courtesy minibus takes less mobile people to the top of the castle site—check when you buy your ticket

💲 Expensive

Greyfriars Kirk

The loyal Greyfriars Bobby sits patiently outside the church and graveyard

THE BASICS

greyfriarskirk.com

+ E7

✉ Greyfriars Kirk, Greyfriars Place EH1 2QQ

☎ 0131 225 1900

🕐 Apr–Oct Mon–Fri 10.30–4.30, Sat 12–4; Nov–Mar variable—check website

🚌 23, 27, 41, 42, 67

♿ Very good

🎟 Free

HIGHLIGHTS

● Greyfriars Bobby
● Elaborate 17th-century memorials
● Peaceful surroundings
● English service at 11 on Sunday and 1.10 on Thursday. Gaelic service at 12.30 on Sunday. All are welcome.

Built in 1620 on the site of the garden of a former Franciscan monastery, the Kirk of the Grey Friars has had a turbulent history. Today it is a peaceful haven for quiet contemplation.

Battleground Just 18 years after the church was built, it was the scene of a pivotal event in Scottish history, when Calvinist petitioners gathered to sign the National Covenant, an act of defiance against the king, Charles I. The church itself was trashed by Cromwell's troops in 1650 and later accidentally blown up. In the kirkyard a makeshift prison was erected to house hundreds of Covenanters captured after the battle of Bothwell Bridge in 1679; they were kept here for five dreadful months. Today it is full of elaborate memorials, including the grave of architect William Adam (1689–1748).

Undying loyalty Opposite the churchyard gate stands a popular Edinburgh landmark: a fountain with a bronze statue of a little Skye terrier, which has stood here since 1873. The dog's story was told by American Eleanor Atkinson in her 1912 novel *Greyfriars Bobby*. He was the devoted companion of a local farmer who dined regularly in Greyfriars Place. After his master died, Bobby slept on his grave in the nearby churchyard for 14 years. A later version suggests he was owned by a local policeman, and taken in by local residents when his owner died. There is a portrait of Bobby, painted by John MacLeod in 1867, inside the church.

The striking National Museum of Scotland incorporates the former Royal Museum

National Museum of Scotland

Here a splendid 19th-century building and an impressive modernist tower that tips its hat to Scotland's baronial architecture stand side by side. Inside are treasures that span millennia.

Much to see With the completion in 2019 of a 15-year renovation, including 13 new galleries, the museum embraces every aspect of Scotland's natural and human history, heritage and geography. Plan to spend at least half a day here. To keep you going, there's the outstanding Tower restaurant on the top floor, or take a picnic up to the roof terrace and enjoy the views.

The highlights The modern wing houses Pictish symbol-stones, Roman and Viking silver, Norse and Celtic jewelry, ivory chess pieces, Jacobite silver and modern sculpture. Don't miss the first-century Hunterston brooch, the beautiful 8th-century Monymusk Reliquary or the mysterious miniature coffins, each containing a tiny human effigy, discovered on Arthur's Seat in 1836. Look out too for the skeleton of a Viking noble who was buried with his tools, weapons and valuables in Orkney.

The new galleries The renovated 19th-century wing houses an eclectic collection, ranging from skeletons of whales and dinosaurs to early aircraft, racing cars and computers. The interactive technology zone between the two wings is great for kids, while the new galleries explore East Asia, Ancient Egypt and Ceramics.

THE BASICS

nms.ac.uk

🔲 E7

✉ Chambers Street EH1 1JF

☎ 0300 123 6789

🕐 Daily 10–5

🍴 Tower restaurant (▷ 44); Balcony Café; Museum Brasserie

🚌 23, 27, 41, 42, 67

♿ Very good

💷 Free; charge for some temporary exhibitions

❓ Check on arrival for times of free daily tours. Free audio guides available in English, Gaelic, French, Spanish, Italian and German

HIGHLIGHTS

- Pictish carvings
- Hunterston brooch
- Lewis chess pieces
- Robbie Burns' pistols
- Eduardo Paolozzi sculptures
- East Asian and Ancient Egypt galleries
- Great views from the roof

Royal Mile

HIGHLIGHTS

● Narrow closes, *wynds* and *vennels* (alleys)
● Tenement houses
● Edinburgh Castle (▷ 24–25)
● Scotch Whisky Experience (▷ 31)
● St. Giles' Cathedral (▷ 30)
● Canongate Kirk (▷ 60)
● Palace of Holyroodhouse (▷ 56–57)

Stretching down from Edinburgh Castle to Holyrood, the Royal Mile is a focal point for visitors, who can explore the narrow *wynds* leading off the main thoroughfare.

Origins The Royal Mile is the long, almost straight street leading up the spine of rock on which the Old Town was built. Lined with medieval tenement houses, this part of the city became so overcrowded that a New Town (▷ 70–71) was built in the 18th century. About 60 narrow closes, or *wynds*, lead off it on either side, whose names, such as Fleshmarket, indicate the trades once carried out there.

Down to earth The Scottish Parliament (▷ 58–59) dominates the Holyrood end of the Royal Mile. From here, the area around

Clockwise from top left: Deacon Brodie's—a traditional pub on the Royal Mile; tartan for sale at shops along the Mile; the Lawnmarket section is lined with gift shops; striking Old Town houses at the back of the Royal Mile

Canongate developed into a more practical, working district. Visit the Museum of Edinburgh (▷ 55) for a glimpse of the interiors of some of the old houses here. Look for a board outside Canongate Kirk (▷ 60) that lists the famous people buried there.

Onward and upward At the crossing of St. Mary's Street and Jeffrey Street you enter High Street. After St. Giles' Cathedral (▷ 30), with the Heart of Midlothian (▷ 33) in the cobbles, the street becomes the Lawnmarket, with its fine 16th- and 17th-century tenements where linen (lawn) was manufactured. On the final stretch above the Hub (a former church that is now headquarters of the Edinburgh Festival) the road narrows on the steep approach to the castle (▷ 24–25).

THE BASICS

✚ C6–H5
✉ The Royal Mile
🚌 23, 27, 41, 42, 67

TIP

● The route has four sections, each with its own identity. You may wish to walk it all in one go or choose to concentrate on one part.

St. Giles' Cathedral

TOP 25

The cathedral's distinctive crown (left); stained glass depicting biblical scenes

THE BASICS

stgilescathedral.org.uk

➕ E6

✉ High Street EH1 1RE

☎ 0131 226 0677

🕐 Mon–Sat 9–5, Sun 1–5 and for services

🍴 St. Giles' Cathedral Café

🚌 23, 27, 41, 42, 67

♿ Very good

💷 Free. A donation of £5 is invited

HIGHLIGHTS

● Robert Louis Stevenson memorial
● Window designed by Edward Burne-Jones
● Robert Burns window
● Stained glass
● John Knox statue
● Medieval stonework

Imposing, and its dark stonework somewhat forbidding, the High Kirk of Edinburgh stands near the top of the Royal Mile. It is dedicated to St. Giles, the patron saint of the city.

Origins of the building The columns inside the cathedral that support the 49m (160ft) tower, with its distinctive crown top, are a relic of the 12th-century church that once occupied this site. The tower itself dates from 1495, and is one of the few remaining examples of 15th-century work to be seen in High Street today. Much of the church has been reworked over subsequent centuries. Don't miss the exquisitely carved 19th-century Thistle Chapel.

Saintly beginnings St. Giles' parish church—it became a cathedral in the mid-17th century—was probably founded by Benedictine followers of Giles. He was a 7th-century hermit (and later abbot and saint) who lived in France, a country with strong ties to Scotland. In 1466, the Preston Aisle of the church was completed, in memory of William Preston, who had acquired the arm bone of the saint in France. This relic disappeared in about 1577, but St. Giles' other arm bone is still in St. Giles' Church, Bruges.

Famous sons Presbyterian reformer John Knox (c.1513–72) became minister here in 1559. You can also see a bronze memorial to writer Robert Louis Stevenson (1850–94), who died in Samoa.

Scotch Whisky Experience

This first-class visitor attraction has matured well since opening in 1988. Various refurbishments have added new features and a fresh approach, creating the perfect blend for the 21st century.

On the whisky trail Take a barrel ride and become part of the whisky-making process. You journey through fields of gently swaying barley and on to the warmth of the malt kiln, with its lingering smell of burning peat. Next stop is the malt mill, followed by the mash tun. Then it's off to the turbulent wooden washback, with the sound of the sloshing wash, before the steaming pot still. Breathe in the smell of the oak casks as the process slows down to the tick-tock of the years of maturation.

Whisky brought to life Characters in costume tell the stories behind the amber liquid and guide you through its development. In the vault you can view the Diageo Claive Vidiz Scotch Whisky Collection, the world's largest collection of Scotch whiskies, and experience the age-old art of "nosing," enabling you to decide if you like fruity, sweet or smoky flavors and to select your perfect dram. The tour concludes with an exhibition charting the humble origins of whisky through to the drink's global success today. Then you can choose from more than 300 types of whisky and liqueurs in the bar.

Too young to drink? Children can enjoy a tour led by Peat, the distillery cat.

THE BASICS

scotchwhiskyexperience.co.uk

✚ D6

✉ 354 Castlehill, The Royal Mile EH1 2NE

☎ 0131 220 0441

🕐 Daily from 10. Closing times vary from 5 to 8.20 depending on time of year

🍴 Amber Restaurant (▷ 42)

🚌 23, 27, 41, 42, 67

♿ Very good

💷 Expensive

HIGHLIGHTS

● Barrel ride
● World's largest collection of Scottish whiskies
● Tasting a dram of your choice
● Children's and specialist tours available

More to See

CAMERA OBSCURA AND WORLD OF ILLUSIONS

camera-obscura.co.uk

At the top of the Royal Mile a castellated building known as the Outlook Tower offers five floors of interactive optical experiences, from illusions to holograms. On the top floor is the camera obscura itself, invented in the 19th century, and like a giant pin-hole camera; it doesn't use film but projects onto a viewing table a fascinating panorama of the city outside (visit on a clear day).

🔒 D6 ✉ Castlehill EH1 2ND ☎ 0131 226 3709 🕐 Opening times vary; generally daily 9–8 or 9 🚌 23, 27, 41, 42, 67 🚻 None 💷 Expensive

CHARLES II STATUE

This splendid memorial to King Charles II is the oldest statue in the city and the oldest equestrian statue in Britain. It was erected in 1685, but the sculptor is unknown.

🔒 E6 ✉ Parliament Square 🚌 23, 27, 41, 42, 67

GLADSTONE'S LAND

nts.org.uk

This restored 17th-century tenement is a highlight in the Old Town. It emphasizes the cramped Old Town conditions—the only space for expansion was up. The building's eventual height of six floors reflects the status of its merchant owner, Thomas Gledstanes. The National Trust for Scotland has re-created 17th-century shop-booths at street level.

🔒 D6 ✉ 477b Lawnmarket EH1 2NT ☎ 0131 226 5856 🕐 Summer daily 10–5; winter daily 11–4.30 🚌 23, 27, 41, 42, 67 🚻 Few; phone for details 💷 Moderate

GRASSMARKET

A long open space below the castle rock, Grassmarket was first chartered as a market in 1477. It was also the site of public executions. A stone marks the location of the old gibbet and commemorates the Covenanting martyrs who died here. Smartened up in recent years, it now has many good shops and

Guarding the entrance to Gladstone's Land

Victoria Street, off Grassmarket

eating places, including the ancient White Hart Inn.

➕ D7 ✉ Grassmarket 🚌 2, 23, 27, 41, 42, 67

HEART OF MIDLOTHIAN

With your back to the entrance of St. Giles' Cathedral, move 20 paces forward and slightly to the right, look down and you will see the outline of a heart in the cobblestones. This Heart of Midlothian marks the place of the old Tolbooth prison, where executions took place.

➕ E6 ✉ High Street EH1 1RE 🚌 23, 27, 41, 42, 67

MEADOW PARK

Known as the Meadows, this area of paths and tree-planted areas makes an ideal place to wander away from the hustle of the city—although not such a good place to be at night. Students, doctors and nurses from the Royal Infirmary and local families all mingle here.

➕ D9 ✉ Meadow Park 🚌 23, 27, 41, 42, 67 ♿ Good

MERCAT CROSS

Located outside St. Giles' Cathedral, the cross was traditionally the location for public declarations, gatherings and executions. The present version, dating from the 1880s, is fashioned on the 17th-century cross, although there may have been a cross here since the 12th century.

➕ E6 ✉ High Street 🚌 23, 27, 41, 42, 67

NATIONAL LIBRARY OF SCOTLAND

nls.uk

This dignified building houses extensive collections of reference works, maps, fiction and non-fiction by Scottish authors and publishers and hosts a year-round calendar of literary exhibitions. Among the 16 million printed items held in 10 subterranean levels, highlights range from the first printed book dedicated to Scottish history, dating from 1527, to official letters from George Washington to Congress, vintage Bartholomew atlases and

The Heart of Midlothian

Mercat Cross

the recently acquired Ian Rankin and Muriel Spark archives, giving a unique insight into these two titans of the Scottish novel.

➕ E6 ✉ George IV Bridge EH1 1EW ☎ 0131 623 3700 🕐 Mon–Tue, Thu 9.30–7, Wed 1–7, Fri–Sat 9.30–5 🚌 23, 27, 41, 42, 67 ♿ Good 🎫 Free

NATIONAL WAR MUSEUM OF SCOTLAND

nms.ac.uk

Exploring more than 400 years of Scottish military history, this museum has displays ranging from major events in Scottish warfare to the personal—diaries, private photographs and belongings of ordinary soldiers. Highlights include a pistol taken from a German spy arrested at Waverley Station in 1940, weaponry, gallantry medals, and even three elephant's toes.

➕ C6 ✉ Edinburgh Castle, Castle Hill EH1 2NG ☎ 0300 123 6789 🕐 Apr–Sep daily 9.45–5.45; Oct–Mar daily 9.45–4.45 🚌 23, 27, 41, 42, 67 ♿ Good 🎫 Expensive (as part of ticket for castle)

PARLIAMENT HOUSE

Home to the law courts, this is the heart of the Scottish legal system. Dating from the 17th century, and restored in 2013, it has a fine hammerbeam roof and a 19th-century stained-glass window. It was home to Parliament from 1639 to 1707 and after devolution between 1999 and 2004.

➕ E6 ✉ Parliament Square EH1 1RQ ☎ 0131 225 2595 🕐 Mon–Fri 9–5 🚌 23, 27, 41, 42, 67 ♿ Good 🎫 Free

THE REAL MARY KING'S CLOSE

realmarykingsclose.com

Remnants of the Old Town's 17th-century houses have been preserved beneath the City Chamber, which was built over the top in 1753. The hour-long underground guided tours bring the close and its people to life.

➕ E6 ✉ 2 Warriston's Close, High Street EH1 1PG ☎ 0131 225 0672 🕐 Apr–Oct daily 10–9; Nov–Mar Sun–Thu 10.15–5.30, Fri–Sat 10.15–9 🚌 23, 27, 41, 42, 67 ♿ Few; phone for details 🎫 Expensive

Checking out the displays in the National War Museum of Scotland

Back in time at the Real Mary King's Close

SURGEONS' HALL MUSEUMS

museum.rcsed.ac.uk

Opened in 1832 on the campus of the Royal College of Surgeons when Edinburgh was at the cutting edge of medical science, Surgeons' Hall Museums is fascinating in a gruesome way. Exhibits include surgical instruments, bone and tissue specimens, one of the world's largest assortments of surgical pathology and a dental collection that will make your teeth twinge. The museum also highlights the criminal careers of Burke and Hare, who notoriously took to murder to make up for a shortfall in cadavers available to medical science in the 1820s.

➕ F7 ✉ Nicolson Street EH8 9DW ☎ 0131 527 1711 🕐 Daily 10–5 🚌 3, 7, , 14, 33 ♿ Good 🎟 Moderate

TALBOT RICE GALLERY

ed.ac.uk

This gallery, within the University of Edinburgh, was established in 1975 and named after art historian David Talbot Rice. It hosts changing exhibitions of the work of international artists and Scottish art, and also commissions new work.

➕ E7 ✉ Old College, South Bridge EH8 9YL ☎ 0131 650 2210 🕐 Tue–Sat 10–5; Aug daily 🚌 3, 7, 8, 14, 33 ♿ Good 🎟 Free

THE WRITERS' MUSEUM

edinburghmuseums.org.uk

The 17th-century Lady Stair's House is home to The Writers' Museum and dedicated to Robert Burns (1759–96), Sir Walter Scott (1771–1832) and Robert Louis Stevenson (1850–94). Scott and Stevenson were both born in Edinburgh and studied law at the university. Particularly significant is Stevenson's memorabilia, as he died abroad and there is no other museum dedicated to him. Contemporary Scottish authors are also represented.

➕ D6 ✉ Lady Stair's Close, Lawnmarket, Royal Mile EH1 2PA ☎ 0131 529 4901 🕐 Daily 10–5 🚌 23, 27, 41, 42, 67 ♿ Phone for details 🎟 Free

The Pathology Museum in the Surgeons' Hall Museums

Robert Burns memorabilia on display at The Writers' Museum

A Wander Around the Old Town

Take in some of the highlights off the beaten track and get a glimpse of the buildings of the Old Town.

DISTANCE: 2km (1.25 miles) **ALLOW:** 45 minutes (but more time with stops)

START

ST. GILES' CATHEDRAL
✠ E6 🚌 23, 27, 35, 41

END

HIGH STREET
✠ E6 🚌 35

❶ Start at the imposing St. Giles' Cathedral (▷ 30) on High Street, with the Mercat Cross (▷ 33) outside. With the cathedral to your left, take the next left over George IV bridge.

❽ Escape the crowds by wandering along some of the old narrow *wynds* (alleys). Continue along Lawnmarket and back to High Street.

❷ Also known as Melbourne Place, this will take you down to the National Museum of Scotland (▷ 27). Cross the road to Greyfriars, at the end of which is Greyfriars Kirk (▷ 26).

❼ Take Granny Green's Steps up to the castle (▷ 24–25). Turn right and follow the castle along until you eventually come to the Hub, a redundant church with a high spire. Cross over into Lawnmarket to soak up the atmosphere of the Old Town.

❸ Turn down Candlemaker Row and keep bearing left until you come into Grassmarket (▷ 32–33).

❻ At the bottom of Grassmarket, in the left-hand corner, take the Vennel, a series of steps up to the city wall, for a good view of the castle. Return to Grassmarket and cross to the far corner.

❹ You can divert here to the right for West Bow, which leads to Victoria Street for specialty shopping and cafés. Return to Grassmarket and look for St. Andrew's Cross.

❺ This is railed and set into the cobbles and is the site of the old gallows.

Shopping

ARMCHAIR BOOKS

armchairbooks.co.uk

"Very neatly alphabetized chaos" is how this delightful den of a secondhand bookshop describes itself. On its shelves you'll find rare gems, beloved classics and unexpected literary treasures.

🚩 C7 ✉ 72–74 West Port EH1 2LE ☎ 0131 229 5927 🚌 2

ARMSTRONGS

armstrongsvintage.co.uk

Established in 1840, museum-like Armstrongs is Scotland's largest vintage emporium, featuring sassy, retro and traditional Scottish clothing. There are also branches at 64–66 Clerk Street, 14 Teviot Place and a pop-up store in Waverley Mall.

🚩 D7 ✉ 83 Grassmarket EH1 2HJ ☎ 0131 220 5557 🚌 2, 23, 27, 41, 42, 67

BILL BABER

billbaber.com

Bill Baber and his partner Helen have been creating beautiful garments since 1977, using yarns of raw and blended silk, organic Irish linen, soft Egyptian cotton and merino wool dyed in Milan.

🚩 D7 ✉ 66 Grassmarket EH1 2JR ☎ 0131 225 3249 🚌 2, 23, 27, 41, 42, 67

SCOTTISH WOOL

If you're looking for the very best in Scottish woolens, you could easily spend a small fortune on designer cashmere in Edinburgh. However, there's also a plethora of factory outlets with good-quality knit-wear at knockdown prices, particularly cashmere, although you are unlikely to find anything leading the way in designer fashion here. Serious knitters will delight in the huge range of yarns available in every conceivable shade, at a good price.

CIGAR BOX

This Royal Mile retailer has achieved the gold standard in Habanos. From famous names like Montecristo and Romeo y Julieta to specialties from Nicaragua, you'll find them here.

🚩 E6 ✉ 361 High Street EH1 1PW ☎ 0131 225 3534 🚌 3, 5, 7, 8, 14, 29, 30, 31, 33, 35, 37, 45, 49

FABHATRIX

fabhatrix.com

This hat shop promotes Scottish designers and many hats are made on the premises. You'll find everything from tweed to trendy fascinators.

🚩 D7 ✉ 13 Cowgatehead EH1 1JY ☎ 0131 225 9222 🚌 23, 27, 41, 42, 67

HAWICO

hawico.com

Cashmere doesn't come cheap and sweaters from this boutique are eye-wateringly expensive; however, the Cashmere Made In Scotland label guarantees the highest quality. The scarves are less pricey.

🚩 D7 ✉ 71 Grassmarket EH1 2HJ ☎ 0131 225 8634 🚌 2, 23, 27, 41, 42, 67

HERMAN BROWN

hermanbrown.co.uk

Just off Grassmarket, Herman Brown has a wealth of hand-picked vintage clothing and accessories.

🚩 C7 ✉ 151 West Port EH3 9DP ☎ 0131 228 2589 🚌 2, 23, 27, 41, 42, 67

IAN MELLIS

mellischeese.net

The range of Scottish cheeses at this cheesemonger's is overwhelming, but staff will help find the perfect cheese for your palate. There are also branches in Morningside and Stockbridge.

🏠 D6 ✉ 30a Victoria Street EH1 2JW
☎ 0131 226 6215 🚌 2, 23, 27, 41, 42, 67

JUST SCOTTISH

justscottishart.com

Here you'll find an eclectic mix of fine and applied art from Scotland's best artists. Choose from fine art, traditional ceramics, beautifully crafted wooden items and a selection of jewelry.

🏠 D6 ✉ 4–6 North Bank Street EH1 2LP
☎ 0131 226 4806 🚌 6, 23, 27, 41, 67

MR WOOD'S FOSSILS

mrwoodsfossils.co.uk

This shop originally supplied museums but now specializes in selling fossils, crystals and minerals from Scotland and all over the world. Knowledgeable and friendly staff will fill you in on Lizzie, at one time the oldest reptile ever discovered.

🏠 D7 ✉ 5 Cowgatehead EH1 1JY ☎ 0131 220 1344 🚌 23, 27, 41, 42, 67

OLD TOWN BOOKSHOP

oldtownbookshop-edinburgh.co.uk

Secondhand books on Scotland and works by Scottish writers, plus music, art and travel fill the shelves here, along with a good range of prints and maps.

🏠 D6 ✉ 8 Victoria Street EH1 2HG ☎ 0131 225 9237 🚌 23, 27, 41, 42, 67

RED DOOR GALLERY

redinburghart.com

This gallery sells original prints, quirky accessories, jewelry and more.

🏠 D6 ✉ 42 Victoria Street EH1 2JW
☎ 0131 477 3255 🚌 23, 27, 41, 42, 67

ROYAL MILE ARMOURIES

heritageofscotland.com

With its impressive-looking replica broadswords, daggers, battle-axes,

helmets and armor, this shop will bring out your inner barbarian and delight fans of *Braveheart*, *Game of Thrones* and *The Lord of the Rings*.

🏠 D6 ✉ 555 Castle Hill EH1 2ND ☎ 0131 225 8580 🚌 23, 27, 41, 42, 67

ROYAL MILE WHISKIES

royalmilewhiskies.com

Enthusiasts are on hand to offer advice on the hundreds of single malt whiskies stocked here—some are 100 years old. Have your items shipped home, or order by phone or online.

🏠 E6 ✉ 379 High Street EH1 1PW ☎ 0131 524 3383 🚌 23, 27, 35, 41, 42

TRANSREAL FICTION

transreal.co.uk

This bookstore is a delight for lovers of science fiction and fantasy. Fans of well-known Edinburgh-based writers like Ken MacLeod and Charles Stross will find signed copies of their latest works here.

🏠 E7 ✉ 46 Candlemaker Row EH1 2QE
☎ 0131 226 6266 🚌 23, 27, 41, 42, 67

Entertainment and Nightlife

BEDLAM THEATRE

bedlamtheatre.co.uk

This 90-seat, student-run theater in a one-time Gothic church is home to Edinburgh University Theatre Company. It presents original and experimental works and is a popular Fringe venue.

🔢 E7 ✉ 11 Bistro Place EH1 1EZ ☎ 0131 629 0430 🚌 23, 27, 35, 45, 47, 300

CABARET VOLTAIRE

thecabaretvoltaire.com

Housed in old subterranean vaults in the Cowgate district, this club is a twin-roomed venue hosting some great gigs. The emphasis here is on electronic music, with popular DJ sessions filling the tiny dance floors.

🔢 E6 ✉ 36–38 Blair Street EH1 1QR ☎ 0131 247 4704 🕐 Most nights (check for times) 🚌 3, 5, 7, 8, 14, 29, 30, 31, 33, 35, 37, 45, 49

CAMEO

picturehouses.co.uk

Cameo, one of the oldest cinemas in Scotland still in use, is a small, comfortable cinema showing the more thoughtful Hollywood hits, plus international and independent films.

🔢 B8 ✉ 38 Home Street EH3 9LZ 🚌 11, 16, 23, 36, 45, X15

EDINBURGH FESTIVAL THEATRE

capitaltheatres.com

This theater, with its distinctive curving glass facade outside and traditional sumptuous decor inside, has one of th largest stages in Europe at 230sq m (2,500sq ft). It hosts a range of dance productions, opera and plays, variety and comedy.

🔢 F7 ✉ 13–29 Nicolson Street EH8 9FT ☎ 0131 529 6000 🚌 3, 5, 7, 8, 14, 29, 30, 3 33, 35, 37, 45, 49

FILMHOUSE

filmhousecinema.com

Opposite the Usher Hall, this art-house cinema has three screens that show the best in art-house and foreign-language cinema from around the globe. Its Café Bar is open until late.

🔢 B7 ✉ 88 Lothian Road EH3 9BZ ☎ 013 228 2688 🚌 1, 10, 11, 16, 24, 34, 36, 47, 12 X5, X15, X24

CELTIC MUSIC

Edinburgh pubs and dinner shows are the best places to track down a genuine Celtic music session. Celtic music originates from the seven Celtic regions—Scotland, Ireland, Wales, Isle of Man, Cornwall, Brittany and Galicia. The following city pubs have fine singers and musicians performing on a regular basis: Sandy Bells Bar (✉ Forrest Road EH1 2QH ☎ 0131 225 2751); The Tass (✉ corner of High Street and St. Mary's Street EH1 1SR ☎ 0131 556 6338); The Royal Oak (✉ Infirmary Street EH1 1LT ☎ 0131 557 2976). Dates and times can be erratic—check first.

FRANKENSTEIN PUB

frankensteinedinburgh.co.uk

In a former Pentecostal church, Frankenstein is a bar, restaurant and club themed to bring a chill to the spine. Have a meal, take a drink in one of the three bars or join a themed part karaoke or games night.

🔢 E7 ✉ 26 George IV Bridge EH1 1EN ☎ 0131 622 1818 🕐 Mon–Thu noon–1am, Fri–Sun noon–2am 🚌 23, 27, 41, 42, 67

THE JAZZ BAR

thejazzbar.co.uk

This intimate, laid-back basement venu serves great cocktails and its musical

menu embraces acoustic blues, funk and soul as well as jazz. There are up to five performances daily.

➕ E7 ✉ 1A Chambers Street EH1 1HR
☎ 0131 220 4298 🚌 3, 5, 7, 8, 14, 29, 30, 31, 33, 35, 37, 45, 49

JOLLY JUDGE

jollyjudge.co.uk

With a log fire and low-beamed ceilings, this characterful 17th-century pub near the foot of the castle offers a wide choice of malt whiskies. It's difficult to find but worth the search.

➕ D6 ✉ 7 James Court, off Lawnmarket EH1 2PB ☎ 0131 225 2669 🚌 23, 27, 41, 42, 67

KING'S THEATRE

capitaltheatres.com

One of Edinburgh's oldest theaters is housed in a handsome Edwardian building. A diverse range of shows and musicals, pantomime, comedy, plays and international opera is performed during the Festival.

➕ C8 ✉ 2 Leven Street EH3 9LQ ☎ 0131 529 6000 🚌 10, 11, 16, 24, 36, 47, X15

QUEEN'S HALL

thequeenshall.net

This venue in a converted church offers a range of events, from jazz and blues to rock and classical music, and comedy from top-class performers. It's home to the Scottish Chamber Orchestra.

➕ F9 ✉ 85–89 Clerk Street EH8 9JG
☎ 0131 668 2019 🚌 2, 3, 5, 7, 8, 29, 30, 31, 33, 37, 47, 49, 300

ROYAL LYCEUM THEATRE

lyceum.org.uk

This magnificent Victorian theater creates all its own shows. Contemporary and classic productions feature, as well as new works.

➕ B7 ✉ 30b Grindlay Street EH3 9AX
☎ 0131 248 4848 (box office) 🚌 1, 10, 11, 16, 24, 34, 36, 47, 124, X5, X15, X24

TRAVERSE THEATRE

traverse.co.uk

This state-of-the-art venue next to the Usher Hall is respected for its experimental plays and dance productions; here you can see hot new work by Scottish playwrights.

➕ B7 ✉ 10 Cambridge Street EH1 2ED
☎ 0131 228 1404 🚌 1, 10, 11, 16, 24, 34, 36, 47, 124, X5, X15, X24

USHER HALL

usherhall.co.uk

Usher Hall is a prestigious concert venue that attracts top performers. The list has included José Carreras, Emeli Sandé, the English Chamber Orchestra and the Moscow Philharmonic.

➕ B7 ✉ Lothian Road EH1 2EA ☎ 0131 228 1155 🚌 1, 10, 11, 16, 24, 34, 36, 47, 124, X4, X15, X24

INTERNATIONAL FILM FESTIVAL

Edinburgh International Film Festival is the longest-running event of its kind in the world, having produced innovative and exciting cinema since 1947. It began with a focus on documentary film, and evolved into a pioneering force for the world of cinema. A celebration of cinema and a showcase for new films from all over the world, it presents UK and world premieres, video shorts and animation. The festival takes place across Edinburgh's cinemas and runs for the last two weeks in June. For information, contact the Edinburgh International Film Festival (✉ 88 Lothian Road EH3 9BZ ☎ box office 0131 228 6382 or 0131 623 8030; edfilmfest.org.uk).

Where to Eat

PRICES

Prices are approximate, based on a 3-course meal for one person.

£££ over £25
££ £15–£25
£ under £15

AMBER RESTAURANT (££–£££)

amber-restaurant.co.uk

In the Scotch Whisky Experience (▷ 31), Amber offers a lunchtime menu of Scottish cuisine for visitors and shoppers. The ambience is transformed in the evening, with soft velvet drapes enclosing a more intimate space to make a romantic setting for a first-class meal. Menus are seasonal and built around locally sourced ingredients.

➕ D6 ✉ 354 Castlehill, The Royal Mile EH1 2NE ☎ 0131 477 8477 ⏰ Sun–Thu noon–8.30, Fri–Sat noon–10 🚌 23, 27, 41, 42, 67

ANGELS WITH BAGPIPES (£££)

angelswithbagpipes.co.uk

A sophisticated restaurant that stands out from the run-of-the-mill eating places in this part of town, Angels with Bagpipes serves imaginative Scottish-fusion dishes. The upstairs dining room looks down on Roxburgh Court, and there's a courtyard where you can eat outdoors on sunny days.

➕ E6 ✉ 343 High Street EH1 1PW ☎ 0131 220 1111 ⏰ Daily noon–10 🚌 23, 27, 41, 42, 67

BENNETS BAR (£)

bennetsbaredinburgh.co.uk

Popular with actors from the nearby King's Theatre (▷ 41), this Victorian bar, adorned with stained glass, tiles, mirrors and carved wood, prides itself on simple, homemade food at a good price, and 100 or so malt whiskies.

➕ B9 ✉ 8 Leven Street EH3 9LG ☎ 0131 229 5143 ⏰ Bar meals Mon–Sat noon–2, 5–8.30 🚌 10, 11, 16, 24, 36, 47, X15

DEACON BRODIE'S TAVERN (££)

nicholsonspubs.co.uk

This traditional pub is a popular spot for locals and visitors alike. Bar snacks are served downstairs, while the upstairs restaurant is more formal. Find out more about the infamous Brodie, one of the inspirations for Stevenson's *Dr. Jekyll and Mr. Hyde*, while you sip your pint.

➕ D6 ✉ 435 Lawnmarket EH1 2NT ☎ 0131 225 6531 ⏰ Mon–Thu noon–midnight, Fri–Sat 11am–1am, Sun 11am–midnight 🚌 23, 27, 41, 42, 67

ELEPHANT HOUSE (£)

elephanthouse.biz

Famous for being the place where J.K. Rowling sat down to write the first Harry Potter story, this popular café offers snacks, light meals and tempting cakes.

➕ E7 ✉ 21 George IV Bridge EH1 1EN ☎ 0131 220 5355 ⏰ Mon–Thu 8am–10pm, Fri 8am–11pm, Sat 9am–11pm, Sun 9am–10pm 🚌 23, 27, 41, 42, 67

TIPS FOR EATING OUT

Many Edinburgh restaurants can seat customers who walk in off the street, but if you have your heart set on eating at a particular establishment, reserve a table in advance. If you pay by credit card, when you key in your PIN you may be prompted to leave a tip. It's acceptable to ignore this and leave a cash tip instead. The normal amount, assuming you are happy with the service, is about 10 percent. In Edinburgh it is fairly common for a reservation to last only a couple of hours, after which time you will be expected to vacate the table for the next sitting.

GRAIN STORE (££–£££)

grainstore-restaurant.co.uk

This smart restaurant has a unique setting in an 18th-century stone-vaulted storeroom with archways and intimate alcoves. Everything on the well-balanced menu is made in house, from the bread to the desserts. The set-price meals are good value for money.

🔲 D6 ✉ 30 Victoria Street (2nd floor) EH1 2JW ☎ 0131 225 7635 🕐 Mon–Sat noon–2.30, 6–9.45, Sun 12.30–9.30 🚌 23, 27, 41, 42, 67

HANAM'S (££)

hanams.com

This restaurant has several colorful rooms over two floors, plus an open-air terrace for summer dining. The menu is authentically Kurdish, with dishes such as *gormeh sabzi* (Persian-style lamb in spinach) and lamb *tashreeb*, a rich spicy stew. Hanam's does not have an alcohol license, but you can bring your own.

🔲 D6 ✉ 3 Johnston Terrace EH1 2PW ☎ 0131 225 1329 🕐 Daily noon–11 🚌 23, 27, 41, 42, 67

INNIS & GUNN BREWERY TAPROOM (£)

innisandgunn.com

This shiny establishment at the western end of the old town offers 26 craft ales on tap, including the Edinburgh-based brewery's own popular beers and a rotating range of other top Scottish craft beers. There's live music every weekend, £5 bar meals served until 5pm and a large all-day menu with several vegan options.

🔲 B7 ✉ 81–83 Lothian Road EH3 9AW ☎ 0131 228 6392 🕐 Mon–Fri 11am–1am, Sat–Sun 10am–1am 🚌 1, 10, 11, 16, 24, 36, 47, 124, X5, X15, X24

THE MITRE (££)

nicholsonspubs.co.uk

Part of a chain that also includes the legendary Deacon Brodie's further up the Mile, the Mitre serves decent pub food (steak-and-ale pie, fish and chips, steak and so on) in an attractive old building. There's a good range of real ales and malt whiskies, too.

🔲 F6 ✉ 133 High Street EH1 1SG ☎ 0131 652 3902 🕐 Mon–Thu noon–midnight, Fri noon–1am, Sat 11am–1am, Sun 11am–midnight 🚌 23, 27, 41, 42, 67

MUMS (££)

monstermashcafe.co.uk

MUMS' subtitle is Great Comfort Food, and the menu is filled with dishes such as sausage and mashed potato, pies and burgers. The bangers come in many varieties, such as Auld Reekie (smoked) and traditional herby pork, and there is a variety of mash to go with them, too. Plastic tomato-shaped ketchup bottles help set the tone.

🔲 E7 ✉ 4a Forrest Road EH1 2QN ☎ 0131 260 9806 🕐 Mon–Sat 9am–10pm, Sun 10–10 🚌 11, 16, 23, 36, 45, X15

ONDINE (£££)

ondinerestaurant.co.uk

Seafood tops the bill at this smart restaurant beneath the stylish Missoni

PUB GRUB

Central-city dining pubs traditionally serve snacks and light meals such as sandwiches, toasted sandwiches, filled potatoes and ploughmans (bread, cheese and pickles). Nowadays, many have extended their menu to include such dishes as curry, steak-and-ale pie, steak and chips or even haggis and neeps (a blend of swede and potato mashed with butter and milk).

Hotel. The hot shellfish platter is a tasty melange of clams, lobster, mussels and langoustines at an eye-popping price. Other good fish options include monkfish and turbot. Service is attentive, and the atmosphere is pleasantly unstuffy.

➕ D6 ✉ 2 George IV Bridge EH1 1AD
☎ 0131 226 1888 🕐 Mon–Sat noon–3, 5.30–10; also Sun in Aug 🚌 23, 27, 41, 42, 67

ONE SQUARE (££–£££)

onesquareedinburgh.co.uk

This modern bar-restaurant close to the theater district is handy for dinner or drinks before or after a show. The menu features classic British cooking based on fine Scottish ingredients, from fillet of sea bream to Ardrossan smoked ham hock. There's a separate vegan menu too.

➕ B7 ✉ 1 Festival Square EH3 9SR ☎ 0131 229 9131 🕐 Mon–Thu noon–10, Fri–Sat noon–10.30, Sun 12.30–5 🚌 1, 10, 11, 16, 24, 34, 36, 47, 124, X5, X15, X24

PETIT PARIS (££)

petitparis-restaurant.co.uk

France meets Scotland at this friendly country-style bistro. The authentic French cooking features regional specialties—for example from Alsace. The restaurant is a member of Slow Food Scotland.

➕ D7 ✉ 38–40 Grassmarket EH1 2JU
☎ 0131 226 2442 🕐 Sun–Fri noon–3, 5–late, Sat noon–late 🚌 2, 23, 27, 41, 42, 67

TOWER RESTAURANT (£££)

tower-restaurant.com

On the fifth floor of the National Museum of Scotland, with great views of the castle, this chic, stylish restaurant offers an interesting selection of eclectic dishes using quality Scottish ingredients, including Dingwall haggis with pineapple salsa and Scottish seafood bouillabaisse.

➕ E7 ✉ National Museum of Scotland, Chambers Street EH1 1JF ☎ 0131 225 3003 🕐 Daily 10–10 🚌 3, 5, 7, 8, 14, 29, 30, 31, 33, 35, 37, 45, 49

WHISKI ROOMS (££–£££)

whiskirooms.co.uk

This world-class whisky bar and bistro offers a choice of 300 single malts and blended whiskies. The menu emphasizes Scottish steaks and seafood, and tempting sticky puddings.

➕ D6 ✉ 4–7 North Bank Street EH1 2LP
☎ 0131 225 7224 🕐 Daily 10am–1am
🚌 6, 23, 27, 41, 67

WITCHERY BY THE CASTLE (£££)

thewitchery.com

This enchanting oak-paneled and candlelit restaurant is the place for a special night out. The cooking adds a contemporary twist to Scottish classics, with signature dishes including Angus beef steak tartare and seafood platters. There is a huge selection of wines.

➕ D6 ✉ Castlehill, Royal Mile EH1 2NF
☎ 0131 225 5613 🕐 Daily noon–11.30
🚌 23, 27, 35, 41, 42

FOOD ON THE RUN

Edinburgh has lots of quick options when you don't want to stop for long. There are food courts in shopping malls, while many attractions have their own restaurants and cafés. American fast-food chains have reached most corners of Scotland, so you won't have to look far to find a pizza or burger, and there are many excellent take-out sandwich bars. Although Edinburgh has many traditional cafés, the word "café" is often used to describe the increasing number of more stylish Continental-style establishments, which bridge the gap between pubs, restaurants and coffee bars.

Canongate and Holyrood

At the east end of the Royal Mile is the Canongate, culminating in the modern Scottish Parliament Building, the Palace of Holyroodhouse and the inviting open space of Holyrood Park.

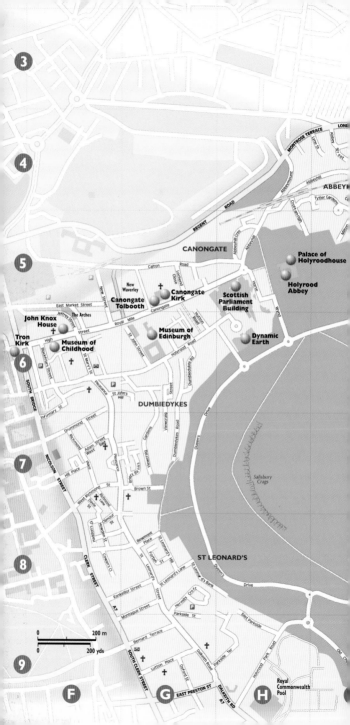

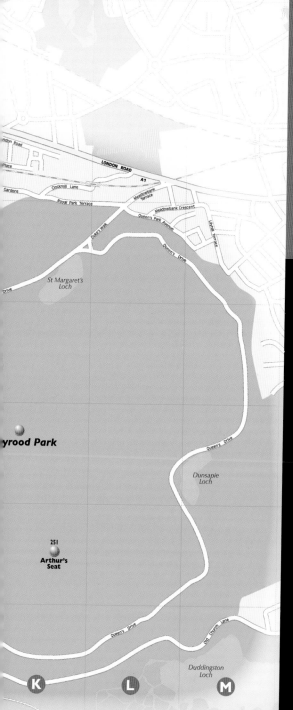

ndon Road

Place

LONDON ROAD

A1

Gardens

Clockmill Lane

Royal Park Terrace

Meadowbank
Terrace

Meadowbank Crescent

Queen's Park Avenue

Lilyhill Terrace

Queen's Walk

Queen's Drive

Drive

St Margaret's
Loch

yrood Park

Queen's Drive

Dunsapie
Loch

251
Arthur's
Seat

Queen's Drive

Old Church Lane

Duddingston
Loch

K   L   M

Arthur's Seat

HIGHLIGHTS

● Spectacular views
● The walk to the top
● Dunsapie Loch and
bird reserve

TIP

● Try to pick a clear day to
get the best from the views.
It's a waste to make the
effort if it's a "dreich" day,
as the Scots call a dismal,
dull day.

**The perfect antidote to the stresses of
the city, with spectacular views, Arthur's
Seat is the remains of an extinct volcano
335 million years old, and it's right on
Edinburgh's doorstep.**

Geological background The green hill of
Arthur's Seat is a city landmark, 251m (823ft)
high and visible for miles. Formed during the
early Carboniferous era, it is surrounded by
seven smaller hills. The summit marks where
the cone erupted and molten rock formed the
high cliffs of Salisbury Crags. During the Ice Age
erosion exposed the twin peaks of Arthur's Seat
and the Crow Hill. There are several explana-
tions for the name; some say it is a corruption
of the Gaelic name for archers, others that the
Normans associated it with King Arthur.

From left: The imposing bulk of Arthur's Seat, as seen from the city's Royal Observatory on Blackford Hill; looking out over the city toward Edinburgh Castle

Get active There is open access to Arthur's Seat, the hills and four small lochs, all of which are part of the Royal Park of Holyrood. You'll find parking at the palace, in Duddingston village and by St. Margaret's Loch and Dunsapie Loch. From the latter it is just a short climb to the top, but a more interesting walk is to hike up from the bottom. Start from a path near St. Margaret's Well, just inside the palace's entrance to the park. The path divides at the start of Hunter's Bog valley but both branches lead to the summit. The right-hand path (closed at the time of writing) will take you along the Radical Road that runs beneath the rock face of the Salisbury Crags. The left path goes through Piper's Walk to the top. From here the whole panorama of Edinburgh, the Firth of Forth, the Pentland hills and the coast lies before you.

THE BASICS

✚ K8
✉ Holyrood Park
🕐 Free access, but no vehicular access to the park (except for Dunsapie Loch) on Sun
🚌 6, 35 and then walk through park
♿ Few

Canongate Tolbooth

THE PEC

HIGHLIGHTS

- The building
- Prison cell
- 1940s kitchen
- Bookbinder's workshop
- Re-created tea room

TIP

- Visit the museum early on in your trip to Edinburgh to give you an insight into the background of the people who made the city what it is today.

Dating from 1591, this French-style Tolbooth has served as both a council chamber and a prison. It now houses the People's Story, a museum of everyday life in the city since the 18th century.

From toll-house to museum The Tolbooth, with its distinctive turreted steeple, is the oldest remaining building in this district and marked the boundary between Holyrood and Edinburgh proper. It served as the council chamber and prison for the independent burgh of Canongate until its incorporation into the city in 1856. The huge boxed clock that projects above the street was added in 1884.

Edinburgh life The building is now home to The People's Story, a museum dedicated to

Clockwise from far left: The turreted Canongate Tolbooth, home to The People's Story museum; trade union banners; the people of Edinburgh on the march in the struggle for the right to vote; the museum sign

...veryday life and times in Edinburgh from the ...8th century up to the present day. Using oral ...istory, written sources and the reminiscences ...f local people, it creates a fascinating insight. ...dulge your senses through the visual displays, ...ounds and smells that evoke life in a prison ...ell, a draper's shop and a bookbinder's work-...hop. See a servant at work and a tramcar ...onductor (a clippie, who clipped the tickets). ...he museum portrays the struggle for improved ...onditions and people's rights, and explores ...e role played by the trades union movement ...nd friendly societies, who looked after their ...embers before the welfare state.

...ime off Check out the places the locals went ...o for such leisure time as they had, such as the ...e-created pub, tearoom and washhouse.

THE BASICS

edinburghmuseums.org.uk

🚲 G5

✉ 163 Canongate EH8 8BN

☎ 0131 529 4057

🕐 Daily 10–5

🚌 35

♿ Good

🎟 Free

❓ Shop stocks a wide range of local social history books

Dynamic Earth

In the jaws of a saber-toothed tiger (left); the Restless Earth exhibit (right)

THE BASICS

dynamicearth.co.uk

✚ H6

✉ 112 Holyrood Road EH8 8AS

☎ 0131 550 7800

🕐 Early Feb–Nov daily 10–5.30 (extended hours in summer); Dec–early Feb Wed–Sun 10–5.30

🍴 The Food Chain café

🚌 35

♿ Excellent

💷 Expensive

❓ Well-stocked gift shop—Natural Selection

HIGHLIGHTS

● Striking building
● Deep Time Machine
● MISSION EARTH
● Tropical Rainforest
● "Submarine trip"
● Restless Earth experience
● 360° ShowDome
● Earthscape Scotland

The tented, spiky roof rising like a white armadillo on the edge of Holyrood Park is Edinburgh's millennium project: a science park that thrills at every turn.

Popular science This interactive spectacular tells the story of the Earth and its changing nature, from the so-called Big Bang (as viewed from the bridge of a space ship in the How It All Started gallery) to the present day (exactly who lives where in the rainforest).

Stunning effects With 12 galleries devoted to the planet, the underlying message is that the world is a fascinating and ever-changing place. Experience the effect of erupting volcanoes, the icy chill of the polar regions and even a simulated earthquake. You may get caught in a humid rainstorm in the Tropical Rainforest. Every 15 minutes the sky darkens, lightning flashes, thunder roars and torrential rain descends. You can travel in the Deep Time Machine, where stars are created using lights and mirrors. A multiscreen flight over mountains and glaciers is a dizzying highlight. Earthscape Scotland is a trip through geological time, while MISSION EARTH, opened in 2019, is an augmented reality exploration into the past, present and future of the planet.

Plenty of stamina Dynamic Earth is a popular, impressive feat of high-tech ingenuity. Hardly a relaxing experience, it's exciting to visit, although peak times are likely to be crowded.

Arthur's Seat, at the heart of Holyrood Park (left); festival time in the park (right)

TOP 25

Holyrood Park

It's a pleasant surprise to discover a city park containing such wild countryside. You'll even find small lochs here.

City's green treasure A royal park since the 12th century, Holyrood Park was enclosed by a stone boundary wall in 1541. Spreading out behind the Palace of Holyroodhouse (▷ 56–57), it extends to some 263ha (650 acres) and is dominated by the great extinct volcano Arthur's Seat (▷ 48–49). It represents a microcosm of Scottish landscape, boasting four lochs, open moorland, marshes, glens and dramatic cliffs, the Salisbury Crags, which inspired Sir Arthur Conan Doyle's novel *The Lost World*.

Get your boots on The park is circled by Queen's Drive, built at the instigation of Prince Albert and closed to commercial vehicles. The area around Dunsapie Loch gives a real sense of remote countryside and is a good spot to start the ascent to Arthur's Seat. It is particularly peaceful here when cars are prohibited on Sunday. All in all, the park is an excellent place to walk, cycle or picnic.

More to see Also in the park is St. Margaret's Well, a medieval Gothic structure near the palace, where a clear spring wells from beneath sculpted vaulting. Above St. Margaret's Loch, a 19th-century artificial lake, are the remains of St. Anthony's Chapel. On the edge of the park is Duddingston village and the attractive Duddingston Loch.

THE BASICS

historicenvironment.scot

✚ K7

✉ Holyrood Park

☎ Holyrood Lodge visitor information center: 0131 557 4685

🕐 Free access, but no vehicular access to the park (except for Dunsapie Loch) on Sun

🚌 6, 35 to palace entrance; other buses to perimeter

♿ Varies; phone for details

✋ Free

❓ Walking routes are available online at historicenvironment.scot and from the Holyrood Lodge information center (by the Scottish Parliament), daily 9.30–3

HIGHLIGHTS

- Arthur's Seat (▷ 48–49)
- Dunsapie Loch
- St. Margaret's Well

Museum of Childhood

Museum sign (left); display at the entrance to Gallery One (right)

THE BASICS

edinburghmuseums.org.uk

➕ F6

✉ 42 High Street, Royal Mile EH1 1TG

☎ 0131 529 4142

🕐 Daily 10–5

🚌 3, 5, 7, 8, 14, 29, 30, 31, 33, 35, 37, 45, 49

♿ Very good

🎫 Free

HIGHLIGHTS

● Extensive toy collection
● Kindertransport bear
● Victorian dolls
● Dolls' houses
● Automata

TIP

● Check in advance for the schedule of regularly changing exhibitions and varied events to get the most out of your visit.

This has been described as "the noisiest museum in the world" and it is popular with both children and adults. Introduce your children to the past and maybe relive it yourself.

Nostalgic pleasure The Museum of Childhood is a delight and claims to be the first museum in the world dedicated to the history of childhood. It was the brainchild of town councillor Joseph Patrick Murray, who argued that the museum was about children rather than for them. Opened in 1955, the collection has grown to display a nostalgic treasure trove of dolls and dolls' houses, train sets and teddy bears. Every aspect of childhood is covered here, from education and medicine to clothing and food. Don't miss the refurbished Gallery One, which explores play and learning through 60 rare objects, including a Fisher-Price Chatter telephone from 1979.

Awakening memories There are older items here, such as Victorian dolls and German automata, but probably the best part is recognizing the objects from your own childhood in the collection of playthings from the 1950s to the 90s here, from Scalextric to the Teletubbie

Founding father Joseph Patrick Murray said that his museum explored a specialized field o social history. From the beginning he put his own mark on the huge array of exhibits, with h slant on informative labels.

Models of Highlanders (left); re-creation of an 18th-century merchant's house (right)

Museum of Edinburgh

Edinburgh's own museum is in Huntly House, a 16th-century home much altered in subsequent centuries and at one time occupied by a trade guild.

Picturesque house Just across the road from the Canongate Tolbooth (▷ 50–51), the building housing the Museum of Edinburgh is distinguished by its three pointed gables. Robert Chambers, a Victorian antiquarian, called Huntly House "the speaking house" owing to the Latin inscriptions on the facade.

What's on show The museum is filled with all those local details that bring the history of a city to life. The collections include maps and prints, silver, glass and a vibrant assortment of old shop signs. There are also fine ceramics and examples of Scottish pottery, as well as items relating to Field Marshal Earl Haig, commander of the British Expeditionary Force in World War I. Of particular interest is the collar and bowl that once belonged to Greyfriars Bobby (▷ 26), together with the original plaster model for the bronze statue of the dog in Candlemaker Row. The family activity area has interactive learning displays to appeal to kids. The museum regularly presents temporary exhibitions drawn from its local history and decorative arts collections.

Historical Covenant Also on show is the original National Covenant signed by Scotland's Presbyterian leadership in 1638, which is one of the city's greatest treasures.

THE BASICS

edinburghmuseums.org.uk

⊞ G6

✉ Huntly House, 142 Canongate, Royal Mile EH8 8DD

☎ 0131 529 4143

🕐 Daily 10–5

🚌 35

♿ Poor

🎟 Free

HIGHLIGHTS

- Huntly House building
- Greyfriars Bobby—collar and bowl
- National Covenant
- Earl Haig memorabilia

Palace of Holyroodhouse

HIGHLIGHTS

● State apartments
● Great Gallery
● Chambers of Mary, Queen of Scots

TIP

● It is best to phone ahead as the palace is closed to visitors whenever a member of the royal family is in residence and security surrounding the building is extremely tight.

Founded as a monastery in 1128, the palace today is the Queen's official residence in Scotland. The pepperpot-towered castle is set against the backdrop of majestic Arthur's Seat, at the foot of the Royal Mile.

Steeped in royal history In the 15th century the palace became a guest house for the nearby Holyrood Abbey (now a scenic ruin), and its name is said to derive from the Holy Rood, a fragment of Christ's Cross belonging to King David I (c.1080–1153). Mary, Queen of Scots stayed here, and a brass plate marks where her Italian favorite, David Rizzio, was murdered in her private apartments in the west tower in 1566. During the Civil War in 1650, the palace was seriously damaged and major

Clockwise from far left: Crowning glory—a royal lantern outside the Palace of Holyroodhouse; a stone unicorn stands guard; the mellow evening light enhances the fairy-tale palace; lion detail on the gates; a view of the palace and Arthur's Seat from Calton Hill

rebuilding was necessary. Bonnie Prince Charlie held court here in 1745, followed by George IV on his triumphant visit to the city in 1822, and later by Queen Victoria en route to Balmoral.

Home and art gallery The palace offers all the advantages of exploring a living space steeped in history and filled with works of art from the Royal Collection. More precious artworks are on view in the stunning Queen's Gallery, by the entrance and opposite the Scottish Parliament. The state rooms, designed by architect William Bruce (1630–1710) for Charles II and hung with Brussels tapestries, are particularly elaborate and ornately splendid. Don't miss the 96 preposterous royal portraits (95 kings and one queen) painted in a hurry by Jacob de Wet in 1684–86, which are hung in the Great Gallery.

THE BASICS

royalcollection.org.uk

➕ H5

✉ Canongate, Royal Mile EH8 8DX

☎ 0131 556 5100

🕐 Apr–Oct daily 9.30–6; Nov–Mar daily 9.30–4.30. May close at short notice

🍴 Café at the Palace

🚌 35, 36

♿ Good

💷 Expensive

❓ Free audio tour available. Gift shop stocks cards, books and china

Scottish Parliament Building

Controversial but never boring, the extraordinary Scottish Parliament Building

THE BASICS

visitparliament.scot

➕ H5

✉ The Scottish Parliament, Holyrood Road EH99 1SP

☎ 0131 348 5200

🕐 Mon–Sat 10–5 except during recess (dates scattered throughout the year—check website)

🍴 Café

🚌 6, 35

♿ Excellent

✋ Free

❓ Four guided tours lasting 1 hour are available on Parliament, Architecture, Photography and Art. Reserve tickets for Public Gallery in advance. The shop sells exclusive items branded to the Scottish Parliament

HIGHLIGHTS

● Architecture
● Exhibition on Scottish Parliament
● Public Gallery

The Scotland Act in 1998 established the first Scottish Parliament since 1707. It has been at this striking modern building since 2004.

Setting the scene From 1999, the Scottish Parliament was housed in buildings around the Royal Mile. Debating took place in the Church of Scotland Assembly at the top of the Mound. The then First Minister Donald Dewar commissioned a new parliament building to be constructed opposite Holyrood Palace, at an original estimated cost of around £40 million. The building was finally opened by the Queen in October 2004, by which time the cost had soared to over £400 million. This expense caused a good deal of controversy, but the resulting building was seen as a success.

No expense spared The innovative and critically acclaimed complex was the work of Barcelona-based architect Enric Miralles. The building is set within landscaped public gardens, against a backdrop of the Salisbury Crags. Inspired by the surrounding scenery, Rennie Mackintosh's flower paintings and upturned boats on the seashore, Miralles wanted to create a building that looked as if it were growing out of the land. The effect is enhanced by copious use of natural materials, with intricate details in oak and sycamore offsetting the granite and smooth concrete finishes. The Debating Chamber, where the 129 members meet, has an impressive oak-beamed ceiling.

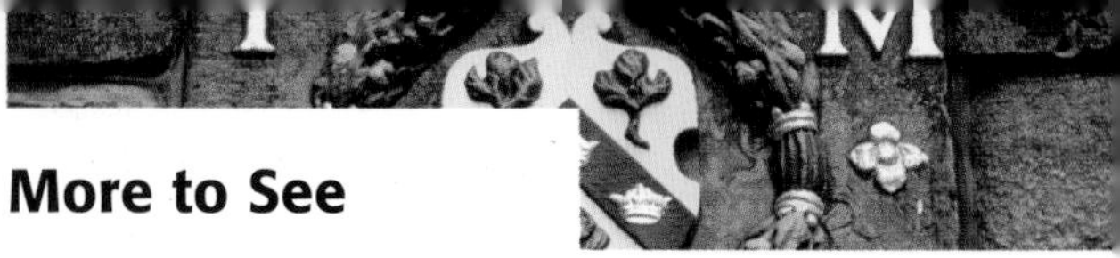

More to See

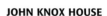

CANONGATE KIRK

canongatekirk.org.uk

Built in 1688, the church's distinctive Dutch gable and plain interior reflect the Canongate's trading links with the Low Countries. Note the gilded stag's head at the gable top, traditionally a gift of the monarch. Buried in the graveyard are economist and philosopher Adam Smith (1723–90) and David Rizzio, darling of Mary, Queen of Scots, murdered in 1566.

G5 Canongate EH8 8BR 0131 556 3515 May–Sep open most days—call ahead to check; Sun services at 11.15 and 6; burial ground open all year 35 Good Free (donations welcomed)

HOLYROOD ABBEY

Founded by King David I in 1128, the present structure was built in the early 13th century. With the reformation the church gradually fell into decline, and it was finally abandoned in 1768, when the roof caved in. You can only see the ruins on a visit to the Palace (▷ 56–57).

JOHN KNOX HOUSE

scottishstorytellingcentre.com

Dating to the 15th century, the house is typical of the period, with overhanging gables and picturesque windows. Inside is a museum with displays relating to Knox and to James Mosman, jeweler to Mary, Queen of Scots. The house is also home to the Scottish Storytelling Centre (▷ 64).

F6 43–45 High Street EH1 1SR 0131 556 9579 Mon–Sat 10–6 (also Sun Jul–Aug) 3, 5, 7, 8, 14, 29, 30, 31, 33, 35, 37, 45, 49 First floor only Inexpensive

TRON KIRK

ewh.org.uk

This fine early Scottish Renaissance church derives its name from the salt-tron, a public weighbeam that once stood outside. The church was deconsecrated in 1952, and is now home to an exhibition focusing on Edinburgh's World Heritage sites.

E6 High Street EH1 2NG 3, 5, 7, 8, 14, 29, 30, 31, 33, 35, 37, 45, 49

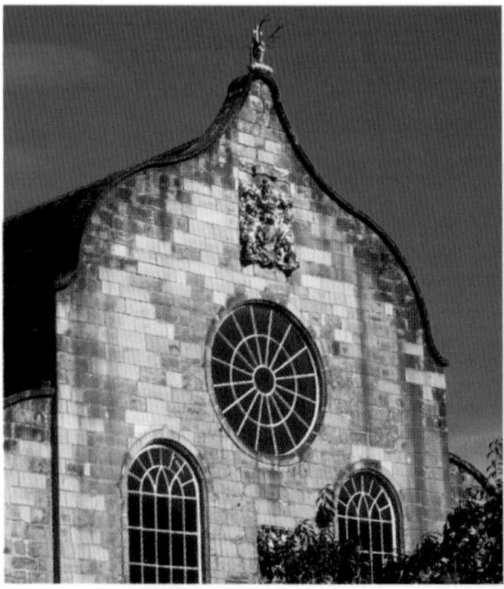

The facade of Canongate Kirk

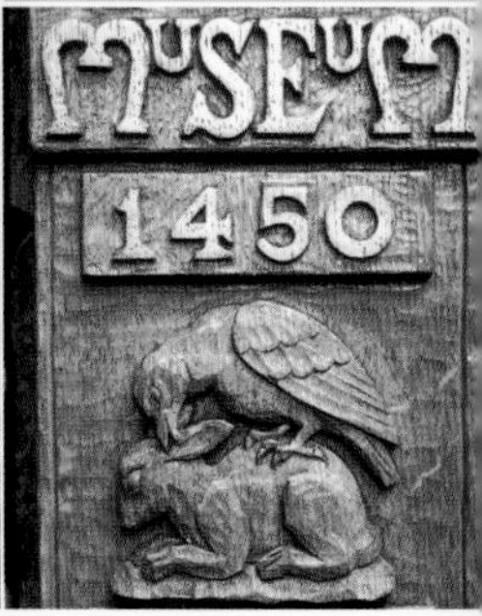

Carved sign on John Knox House

Through Canongate to Holyrood Park

Walk along High Street to Canongate, with its historic buildings and museums, and then take a break in the glorious Holyrood Park.

DISTANCE: 1.5km (1 mile) **ALLOW:** 1 hour (plus time in the park)

START

TRON KIRK
E6 35 and all North Bridge buses

END

HOLYROOD PARK
K7 35

1 Start at the Tron Kirk (▷ 60) on High Street at the junction with South Bridge. Leaving the church to your right, walk up High Street.

8 There are some 263ha (650 acres) to explore here, as well as Dynamic Earth (▷ 52) science park and Arthur's Seat (▷ 48–49).

2 On your left is the John Knox House (▷ 60) and opposite the Museum of Childhood (▷ 54). Continue on into Canongate.

7 Opposite the Parliament, at the end of Canongate (also the end of the Royal Mile), is Holyroodhouse (▷ 56–57), with its fine collection of art and royal objects. Behind the palace is the huge expanse of the delightful Holyrood Park (▷ 53).

3 After about 400m (440yd) you will come to the Museum of Edinburgh (▷ 55) on your right, which gives a good insight into the city's history.

6 Continue toward the end of Canongate and you will see the Scottish Parliament Building (▷ 58–59) on the right, deemed an architectural masterpiece by some but an extravagance by others.

4 On the left, a short distance on, is the old Canongate Tolbooth (▷ 50–51), which houses The People's Story, giving more background to life in historic Edinburgh.

5 Just beyond is Canongate Kirk (▷ 60), the striking Dutch-style church.

Shopping

CRANACHAN & CROWDIE

cranachanandcrowdie.com

The perfect place to pick up a few presents to take home, this tempting emporium is piled high with Scottish delicacies, from whisky to shortbread.

F6 ✉ 263 Canongate EH8 8BQ ☎ 0131 556 7194 🚌 35

FUDGE KITCHEN

fudgekitchen.co.uk

This shop offers 17 different varieties of delectable fudge (including six vegan flavors), all handcrafted using traditional methods and the finest ingredients from a recipe dating from 1830.

F6 ✉ 30 High Street EH1 1TB ☎ 0131 558 1517 🚌 3, 5, 7, 8, 14, 29, 33, 35, 37, 45

GEOFFREY (TAILOR) KILTMAKERS

geoffreykilts.co.uk

This family-run business produces kilts and related items for men and women, either off the peg or made to measure. You can even design your own tartan. All items are made from high-quality materials in Scotland.

F6 ✉ 59 High Street EH1 1SR ☎ 0131 557 0256 🚌 3, 5, 7, 8, 14, 29, 33, 35, 37, 45

NEANIE SCOTT

Unlike many of the Royal Mile giftshops, Neanie Scott's range of souvenirs, crafts and weapons is mainly made in Scotland. The friendly proprietor is always ready to chat to visitors and offe advice on purchases.

G5 ✉ 131 Canongate EH8 8BP ☎ 013 558 3528 🚌 35

PALENQUE

palenquejewellery.co.uk

Palenque specializes in competitively priced, high-quality contemporary silver rings, necklaces, pendants and bracelet and handcrafted accessories.

F6 ✉ 56 High Street EH1 1TB ☎ 0131 557 9553 🚌 3, 5, 7, 8, 14, 29, 33, 35, 37, 45

RAGAMUFFIN

Displays of vivid handmade chunky knitwear, scarves, accessories and toys catch your eye in the huge windows of this stylish boutique on the corner of St. Mary's Street.

F6 ✉ 278 Canongate EH8 8AA ☎ 0131 557 6007 🚌 35

UNKNOWN PLEASURES

vinylnet.co.uk

A treasure trove for any collector of vin records, this little shop stocks rare and desirable recordings from artistes rang- ing from multimillion-sellers to the delightfully obscure.

G5 ✉ 110 Canongate EH8 8DD ☎ 013 652 3537 🚌 35

WILLIAM CADENHEAD

wmcadenhead.com

This quaint shop, hidden at the bottom of the Royal Mile, advertises itself as Scotland's oldest independent bottler and specializes in malt whiskies, old oak-matured Demerara rum and—since 2019—cognac and calvados.

G6 ✉ 172 Canongate EH8 8DF ☎ 0131 556 5864 🚌 35

BAGPIPES

The bagpipes are synonymous with Scotland. You see them everywhere, from the Military Tattoo in Edinburgh to school sports days and agricultural shows. There are many types, played in countries all over the world but often associated with the military. Surprisingly, the bagpipes' origins are not even Scottish but possibly ancient Egyptian or Greek.

Entertainment and Nightlife

BONGO CLUB

thebongoclub.co.uk

A peripatetic venue founded in the 1990s by young local artists and performers, Bongo is the place to go for DJ sets and live music.

➕ E7 ✉ 66 Cowgate EH1 1JX ☎ 0131 558 8844 🕐 Tue–Sat 10pm–3am (but times can vary) 🚍 3, 5, 7, 8, 14, 29, 33, 35, 37, 45, 49

SCOTTISH STORYTELLING CENTRE

scottishstorytellingcentre.com

This venue stages Scottish and children's plays, and story and poetry readings.

➕ F6 ✉ 43–45 High Street EH1 1SR ☎ 0131 556 9579 🕐 Mon–Sat 10–6, Sun (Jul–Aug only) 12–6 🚍 3, 5, 7, 8, 14, 29, 33, 35, 37, 45 ♿ Good 🎫 Some events free

WAVERLEY BAR

The walls and ceiling of this tiny, quirky, old-fashioned bar are plastered with posters from long-forgotten bands and Fringe performances. It still hosts live folk music on Friday evenings and Sunday afternoons.

➕ F6 ✉ 1 St. Mary's Street EH1 1TA ☎ 01 557 1050 🕐 Daily 7–11pm (sometimes later during Festival) 🚍 35 🎫 Free

WHISTLEBINKIES

whistlebinkies.com

This local favorite offers live music (mainly rock and folk) every night.

➕ F6 ✉ 4–6 South Bridge EH1 1LL ☎ 01 557 5114 🕐 Daily 5pm–3am (exact performance times vary) 🚍 3, 5, 7, 8, 14, 29, 30, 3 33, 35, 37, 45, 49 🎫 Free

Where to Eat

THE CANONS' GAIT (££)

gait.bar

This lively gastropub offers a good selection of Scottish real ales and an imaginative range of dishes, from Japanese katsu chicken salad and burgers to spiced vegetable tagine.

➕ F6 ✉ 232 Canongate EH8 8DQ ☎ 0131 556 4481 🕐 Meals Mon–Thu noon–9, Fri–Sun noon–10; bar Mon–Thu 11–11, Fri–Sat noon–midnight 🚍 35

DAVID BANN (££)

davidbann.co.uk

David Bann's well-designed restaurant makes good use of natural wood and soft lighting to set the mood for mode vegan and vegetarian cuisine.

✉ F6 ✉ 56–58 St. Mary's Street EH1 1SX ☎ 0131 556 5888 🕐 Mon–Fri noon–10, Sat–Sun 11–10 🚍 35

DUBH PRAIS RESTAURANT (££)

hewatsedinburgh.com

Seek out this romantic cellar restauran for Scottish fare such as sea bass, sirlc steak, chicken, pork belly and wild mushroom tortellini.

➕ F6 ✉ 123b High Street EH1 1SG ☎ 01 557 5732 🕐 Mon–Sat 5–9.30, Sun 6–9; also Sat noon–2.30 🚍 23, 27, 41, 42, 67

New Town

The New Town displays Edinburgh's elegant face. The broad Georgian streets are lined with gracious houses with large windows and handsome doorways. Here, too, is where you will find the best shopping and eating opportunities.

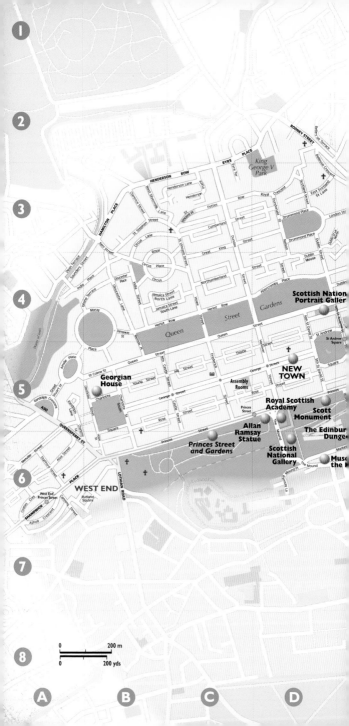

Calton Hill

The attractive array of Classical buildings on Calton Hill

THE BASICS

edinburghmuseums.org.uk
+ F4
X26
Edinburgh Museums and Galleries
0131 556 2716

HIGHLIGHTS

● Spectacular views
● Nelson Monument
● National Monument
● City Observatory
● Playfair Monument
● Dugald Steward Monument

Remarkable buildings grace the top of this volcanic hill, and it is also worth the climb for superb views over the city—Robert Louis Stevenson's most-loved vista of Edinburgh.

Grandiose style Calton Hill (108m/354ft) is crowned by the columns of one of Edinburgh's more eccentric edifices. In 1822 work began on the National Monument of Scotland. Inspired by the Parthenon in Athens and built by public subscription, it was to be a monument to Scottish sailors and soldiers killed in the Napoleonic Wars, but in 1829—with only 12 columns completed—the money ran out. The prolific Edinburgh architect William Playfair grandiose monument became known as "Edinburgh's Disgrace." The remaining folly, however, is part of the distinctive skyline of Calton Hill.

Other monuments Sharing the slopes of Calton Hill with the National Monument are the City Observatory (designed by James Craig) and the Dugald Steward Monument, commemorating the well-known philosopher, another design by William Playfair. Also on the hill is the 1816 tower of the Nelson Monument, a 143-step climb, but worth the effort. The climb to the park at the top is rewarded by superb view. Here on the grassy slopes you can see south to the red-toned cliffs of Salisbury Crags and down to the undulating slopes of Holyrood Park or to the east beyond Princes Street.

Robert Adam's Georgian House (right) has some classic 18th-century displays (left)

Georgian House

This elegant house, with its preserved period interiors, gives you a fascinating glimpse into the lives of the prosperous classes who lived in the New Town in the 18th century.

How the other half lived The north side of Charlotte Square is the epitome of 18th-century New Town elegance and was designed by architect Robert Adam (1728–92) as a single, palace-fronted block. With its symmetrical stonework, rusticated base and ornamented upper levels, it is an outstanding example of the style. The Georgian House, a preserved residence on the north side of the square, oozes gracious living. It is a meticulous re-creation by the National Trust for Scotland, reflecting all the fashionable details of the day, right down to the Wedgwood dinner service on the dining table and the magnificent drawing room with its beautiful candlesticks.

Georgian elegance As you step in the door of this house you can't help but be impressed by the balustraded staircase and its stunning cupola above, flooding the building with light. The stairs lead to the second floor and the Grand Drawing Room, perfect for entertaining.

Below stairs For a contrast, take a look in the basement at the well-scrubbed kitchen and storage areas, including the wine cellar and china closet. Here the hard work took place, reflecting the marked social divides of the time.

THE BASICS

nts.org.uk

⊞ B5

✉ 7 Charlotte Square EH2 4DR

☎ 0131 226 3318

🕐 First 3 weeks Mar, Nov daily 11–3.15; late Mar–Oct daily 10–4.15; Dec–Feb Wed–Sun 11–3.15

🚌 19, 36, 41, 43, 47, 104, 113, X5, X7, X37, X43, X47

♿ Limited; six steps to first floor

👆 Moderate

HIGHLIGHTS

● Staircase and cupola
● Grand Drawing Room
● Dining Room
● Basement with kitchen

HIGHLIGHTS

- Charlotte Square
- The Georgian House
  (▷ 69)
- The Mound

A product of the lack of space in Edinburgh's Old Town, this spectacular piece of Georgian town planning was instigated by a competition in 1766 to build a fine "New Town."

Georgian streets Edinburgh's so-called New Town covers an area of about 318ha (1sq mile) to the north of Princes Street, and is characterized by broad streets of spacious terraced houses with large windows and ornamental door arches. The original area comprised three residential boulevards to run parallel with the Old Town ridge: Princes Street, George Street and Queen Street. With a square at each end (St. Andrew and Charlotte), they were also linked by smaller roads—Rose Street and Thistl Street—to shops and businesses. While Princes

Clockwise from far left: The entrance to this 18th-century house in New Town looks a picture with its floral display; townhouse rooftop detail; typical Georgian fanlight and porch, and ornate lamp outside; created from a huge pile of rubble, the Mound went on to support Edinburgh's most prestigious art galleries

Street has been taken over by commercial activity, wide Charlotte Square, with its preserved Georgian House (▷ 69), is the epitome of the planners' intentions.

Other highlights It took 2 million cartloads of rubble to create the Mound, later home to the Scottish National Gallery (▷ 72–73) and the Royal Scottish Academy (▷ 76). The Mound came about by accident when clothier "Geordie" Boyd started to dump rubble in the marsh, quickly followed by the builders from New Town. Farther out is Stockbridge, a former mining village developed as part of a second New Town. It was on land owned by the painter Sir Henry Raeburn and became a bohemian artisans' corner. Ann Street is now one of the city's top addresses (▷ 99).

THE BASICS

🔁 D5
ℹ️ Edinburgh iCentre, 249 High Street EH1 1YJ
☎ 0131 473 3868

Scottish National Gallery

TOP
25

● *The Revd Dr Robert Walker Skating on Duddingston Loch* by Sir Henry Raeburn
● Monet's *Haystacks*
● Botticelli's *Virgin Adoring the Sleeping Christ Child*
● Land- and seascapes by William McTaggart
● Works by Old Masters, including Vermeer, Raphael and Titian

This striking 19th-century building houses superb Old Masters and an outstanding Scottish collection. It is the perfect setting for Scotland's finest art.

Artistic venue The gallery was designed by New Town architect William Playfair (1790–1857) and completed in the year of his death. It is easily spotted thanks to the huge golden stone pillars of its neoclassical flanks and should not be confused with the nearby Royal Scottish Academy, which has been refurbished as an international exhibition venue (▷ 76).

What's on show The gallery's impressive collection of paintings, sculptures and drawings includes more than 20,000 items, displayed in intimate and accessible surroundings. The time

Clockwise from far left: Botticelli's Virgin Adoring the Sleeping Christ Child, *c.1490; busts on the gallery stairs; Lorenzo Bartolini's graceful sculpture* The Campbell Sisters *(1821; Monet's* Haystacks: Snow Effect, *1891; Raeburn's* The Revd Dr Robert Walker Skating on Duddingston Loch, *c.1795; the gallery facade*

pan runs from the early Renaissance to the end of the 19th century. At the collection's heart are paintings by the great masters of Europe, including Vermeer, Van Gogh, Raphael and Titian. Look out for Monet's *Haystacks* (1891), Velázquez's *Old Woman Cooking Eggs* (1618) and Botticelli's masterpiece *Virgin Adoring the Sleeping Christ Child* (c.1490).

Scottish contingent Not surprisingly, the gallery has an outstanding collection of works by Scottish artists. Favorites include Raeburn's c.1795 portrait of *The Revd Dr Robert Walker Skating on Duddingston Loch,* and the sweeping land- and seascapes of William McTaggart. Look also for the vivid scenes of everyday life among the common people, as captured on canvas by Sir David Wilkie.

THE BASICS

nationalgalleries.org

✚ D6

✉ The Mound EH2 2EL

☎ 0131 624 6200

🕐 Daily 10–5, Thu until 7

🍴 Café

🚌 6, 23, 27, 41, 67 and tram; a free bus links the National Gallery with the Gallery of Modern Art

♿ Good

🎟 Free; charge for some exhibitions

❓ Shop stocks cards, books and gifts (▷ 80)

Princes Street and Gardens

TOP
25

The Ross fountain in Princes Street Gardens (left); fountain detail (right)

THE BASICS

✚ C6

✉ Princes Street EH2 2HG

☎ 0131 529 7921

🕐 Gardens: summer 7am–around 10pm; winter 7–around 6

✋ Free

HIGHLIGHTS

● Great views to the castle
● Jenners department store (▷ 79)
● Floral clock
● Summer band concerts

Originally designed as a residential area, the most famous street in Scotland is now where local people come to shop. The gardens are a welcome escape from the urban buzz.

Changes over time If you stroll along Queen Street, you can see how it echoes Princes Street and gives an insight into James Craig's original residential plan. He designated today's Thistle and Rose streets, lesser byways between the grand thoroughfares, as the living and business place of tradespeople and shopkeepers. The use of the lanes behind Thistle and Rose street to reach the back doors of the wealthier residents was a clever element in his scheme. By the mid-19th century developments began to encroach, however, and the gracious Georgian buildings started to deteriorate, some replaced by more utilitarian edifices in the 20th century.

Getting its name Princes Street was originally to be called St. Giles Street, but King George III objected as it reminded him of the St. Giles district of London, which was notorious for its lowlife. The street instead became Princes Street after his two eldest sons.

Oasis of green Princes Street Gardens are a pleasant place to sit down and admire the backs of the Old Town tenements across the valley. In summer there are concerts to enjoy and, an Edinburgh institution since 1902, the floral clock—a flowerbed planted up as a clock.

More to See

ALLAN RAMSAY STATUE

In West Princes Street Gardens is a statue of the former wig-maker turned poet Allan Ramsay (1686–1758), by Sir John Steell (1850).

🔼 D5 ✉ West Princes Street Gardens 🚍 1, 10, 11, 16, 24, 34, 36, 47, 124, X5, 15, X24

CITY ART CENTRE

edinburghmuseums.org.uk
The gallery is housed in a six-floor former warehouse. It stages changing exhibitions and displays the city's collection of Scottish paintings, including works by the 20th-century Scottish Colourists.

🔼 E6 ✉ 2 Market Street EH1 1DE ☎ 0131 29 3993 🕐 Daily 10–5 🍴 Café 🚍 All buses to Waverley Station 🚹 Very good 🎫 Free; charge for some exhibitions

CITY OBSERVATORY AND CITY DOME

collective-edinburgh.art
The old City Observatory on Calton Hill reopened in 2017 and is now fully open to the public for the first time, housing a restaurant and visual arts space. The observatory complex also comprises the City Dome, a venue for art exhibitions.

🔼 F4 ✉ 38 Calton Hill EH7 5AA ☎ 0131 556 1264 🕐 Apr–Oct Tue–Sun 10–5; Nov–Mar Tue–Sun 10–4; restaurant Mon 5–9.30, Tue–Sun 10–9.30 🚍 X5, X7, X15, X17, X18, X25, X26, X27, X28, X44 🚹 Good 🎫 Free

THE EDINBURGH DUNGEON

thedungeons.com
Beneath the paving stones of the city, take a tour to encounter witch-hunters, cannibals and murderers, including Edinburgh's most notorious serial killers, Burke and Hare. It's not recommended for the faint-hearted or very young children.

🔼 E6 ✉ 31 Market Street EH1 1DF ☎ 0131 240 1001 🕐 Times vary; check website 🚍 All buses to Waverley Station 🚹 Phone for details 🎫 Expensive

GENERAL REGISTER HOUSE

nrscotland.gov.uk
Register House was originally sited in the castle, then in the Tolbooth,

The City Observatory complex

until it acquired a custom-built home in Princes Street in 1774 to house the national archives. It is guarded by a famous statue of the Duke of Wellington.

➕ E5 ✉ Scottish Record Office, 2 Princes Street EH1 3YY ☎ 0131 535 1314 🕐 Mon–Fri 9–4.30 🚌 All buses to Waverley Station ♿ Very good 🎫 Free with reader's ticket; proof of identity required

MUSEUM ON THE MOUND

museumonthemound.com

Located in the Bank of Scotland's headquarters, this small, unusual museum displays old maps, gold coins, bank notes, forgeries and bullion chests.

➕ D6 ✉ The Mound EH1 1YZ ☎ 0131 243 5464 🕐 Tue–Fri 10–5, Sat 1–5 🚌 23, 27, 41, 42, 67 ♿ Good 🎫 Free

ROYAL SCOTTISH ACADEMY

royalscottishacademy.org

William Playfair's lovely classical building is now linked to the National Gallery to create a superb space for displaying art.

➕ D5 ✉ The Mound EH2 2EL ☎ 0131 225 6671 🕐 Mon–Sat 10–5, Sun noon–5 🚌 6, 23, 27, 41, 42, 67; free bus links main galleries ♿ Very good 🎫 Free; charge for some exhibitions

SCOTT MONUMENT

edinburghmuseums.org.uk

Generations have climbed this 61m (200ft) structure since it opened in 1846 to appreciate fine views of the city. The stone figures are characters from Sir Walter Scott's novels.

➕ D5 ✉ East Princes Street Gardens EH2 2EJ ☎ 0131 529 4068 🕐 Daily 10–5 🚌 All buses to Waverley Station 🎫 Moderate

SCOTTISH NATIONAL PORTRAIT GALLERY

nationalgalleries.org

This gallery tells the history of Scotland through the portraits of the great, the bad and the vain.

➕ D4 ✉ 1 Queen Street EH2 1JD ☎ 0131 624 6200 🕐 Daily 10–5 🚌 24, 29, 42; free bus links main galleries ♿ Very good 🎫 Free; charge for some exhibitions

The Scottish National Portrait Gallery

Georgian Facades
of New Town

Explore New Town's streets and squares, full of superb Georgian architecture. For shopping, try George Street and Multrees Walk.

DISTANCE: 4km (2.5 miles) **ALLOW:** 1 hour 30 minutes, plus stops

START

PRINCES STREET
🚇 D5 🚌 3, 10, 17, 25, 44

1 Start on Princes Street (▷ 74) by the Royal Scottish Academy (▷ 76). Cross over into Hanover Street. Take the second turning on your left and walk along George Street.

2 At the end is Charlotte Square, one of the finest examples of Georgian architecture in the city. Turn right and right again into Young Street. At the end turn left and go down North Castle Street.

3 When you reach Queen Street cross over and turn left, then take the next right down Wemyss Place. Turn right into Heriot Row.

4 Here you will find the home of Robert Louis Stevenson. When you reach Howe Street turn left and take the second left into South East Circus Place.

END

PRINCES STREET
🚇 D5 🚌 3, 10, 17, 25, 44

8 In front of you is St. Andrew Square. Go around the square, turning left into North St. David Street, which leads back to Princes Street.

7 At the roundabout turn right and walk up Broughton Street, with its good choice of refreshment stops. At the end of the street turn right onto York Place and then turn left onto Elder Street. Take the next right down Multrees Walk (▷ 79, panel).

6 At the end turn right onto St. Vincent Street. Cross over into Great King Street and at the end turn right and then immediately left onto Drummond Place and continue ahead into London Street.

5 Pause to admire the sweep of the Royal Circus before you bear right for North East Circus Place.

Shopping

21ST CENTURY KILTS

21stcenturykilts.com

Howie Nicholsby is on a one-man campaign to bring the kilt into the 21st century. His practical, contemporary kilts and three-button jackets have made him popular across Europe.

➕ C5 ✉ 48 Thistle Street EH2 1EN ☎ 0131 225 1662 🚌 23, 24, 27, 29, 42

ANTHONY WOODD GALLERY

anthonywooddgallery.com

Traditional art—mainly 19th-century oils, watercolors and prints, from landscapes to sporting and military subjects—is the focus here.

➕ C4 ✉ 4 Dundas Street EH3 6HZ ☎ 0131 558 9544/5 🚌 23, 27

BISCUIT

biscuit.clothing

This welcoming store offers up an eclectic mix of women's clothing to inspire and delight, along with beautiful things for the home, including cushions, candles and decorations.

➕ D5 ✉ 22 Thistle Street EH2 1EN ☎ 0131 225 2308 🚌 6, 23, 27, 67

THE BON VIVANT'S COMPANION

bonvivantscompanion.co.uk

A liquor store where knowledgable staff are passionate about a good tipple. The shelves brim with more than 300 carefully selected wines, a wide range of Scottish craft beers and 40 rare and interesting gins.

➕ C5 ✉ 51 Thistle Street EH2 1DY ☎ 0131 225 6055 🚌 23, 24, 27, 29, 42

CARSON CLARK

carsonclarkgallery.co.uk

This gallery has moved west across town but still specializes in wonderful antique maps and sea charts from all over the globe, dating from the 16th to the 19th centuries, as well as replica maps and reproduction prints.

➕ C4 ✉ 34 Northumberland Street EH3 6LS ☎ 07980 874227 🚌 23, 27

CONCRETE WARDROBE

concretewardrobe.com

This store specializes in clothes, accessories and crafts by local designer and 20th-century collectibles from the 1920s to the 1970s.

➕ E3 ✉ 50A Broughton Street EH1 3SA ☎ 0131 558 7130 🚌 1, 4, 5, 7, 8, 14, 19, 22 25, 34, 45, 49

CURIOUSER AND CURIOUSER

curiouserandcuriouser.com

Curiouser and Curiouser sells attractive prints and paintings by Scottish artists, illustrated books, pottery, jewelry and colorful cards, toys and accessories.

➕ E3 ✉ 93 Broughton Street EH1 3RZ ☎ 0131 556 1866 🚌 1, 4, 5, 7, 8, 14, 19, 22 25, 34, 45, 49

THE EDINBURGH BOW TIE CO.

Until recently only worn by the frightful posh or the endearingly eccentric, the bow tie is making its way back into the mainstream. This dedicated store sells a wide range, and you can even design your own and have it made up for you.

➕ C5 ✉ 67 Rose Street EH2 2NH ☎ 0131 343 2763 🚌 25, 26, 44 and tram

HAMILTON & INCHES

hamiltonandinches.com

Established in 1866, the city's most reputable jeweler offers imaginative jewelry and silverware in a grand old building with workshops above and an ornate interior, complete with chandeliers.

➕ C5 ✉ 87 George Street EH2 3EY ☎ 0131 225 4898 🚌 10, 11, 12, 16, 41, 42

HANOVER HEALTH FOODS
hanoverhealth.co.uk

Edinburgh's oldest health food store—it's been going since 1904—is a handily located and friendly place to pick up vitamins, herbs and supplements. They also stock organic wholefoods and snacks, and healthy products for skin and body.

🔲 D5 ✉ 40 Hanover Street EH2 2DR
☎ 0131 225 4291 🚌 6, 23, 27, 67

HENDERSONS SHOP AND DELI
hendersonsofedinburgh.co.uk

This shop on the corner of Thistle Street dates from the 1960s and is the city's original farm shop. Today it still sells freshly harvested organic produce from Janet Henderson's farm in East Lothian. You can also walk out with a vegetarian or vegan meal prepared in house to one of Henderson's classic recipes, or take a seat and eat in.

🔲 D5 ✉ 92 Hanover Street EH2 1DR
☎ 0131 225 6694 🚌 6, 23, 27, 67

JANE DAVIDSON
janedavidson.co.uk

Jane's daughter Sarah has built her reputation on providing excellent service. The three-floor Georgian town house stocks exclusive cashmere labels from around the world and features many top designers, such as Allegra Hicks and Diane Von Furstenberg.

🔲 C5 ✉ 52 Thistle Street EH2 1EN ☎ 0131 225 3280 🚌 6, 23, 27, 67

JENNERS
houseoffraser.co.uk

Edinburgh's grand old dame was founded in 1838—making it the oldest independent department store in the world until it was taken over by House of Fraser. The magnificent building is a rabbit warren inside, with a central galleried arcade, and houses over 100 departments, from clothes and shoes to perfume, glassware, groceries and toys. There are four cafés, including the excellent Valvona & Crolla VinCaffè bar and restaurant (▷ 86).

🔲 D5 ✉ 47–48 Princes Street EH2 2YJ
☎ 0343 909 2031 🚌 All buses to Waverley Station, and tram

JOSEPH BONNAR
josephbonnar.com

In business since the 1960s, Joseph Bonnar boasts Scotland's largest range of antique jewelry, plus other items.

🔲 C5 ✉ 72 Thistle Street EH2 1EN ☎ 0131 226 2811 🚌 6, 23, 27, 67

LINZI CRAWFORD
linzicrawford.com

The only stockist of several edgy European labels, Linzi also has her own line of merino and cashmere clothing in distinctive shades.

🔲 D4 ✉ 27 Dublin Street EH3 6NL ☎ 0131 558 7558 🚌 10, 11, 12, 16, 26, 44

MCNAUGHTAN'S BOOKSHOP
mcnaughtansbookshop.com

At this highly respected secondhand and antiquarian bookshop, casual browsing

WALK THE WALK

Multrees Walk is a great place for designer shopping in Edinburgh (the-walk.co.uk). The stylish pedestrianized shopping street has attracted a whole host of prestigious international retailers, such as Links of London, Mulberry, Azendi, Calvin Klein, Louis Vuitton, Emporio Armani and Boss. It also boasts a five-floor Harvey Nichols department store, several stylish accessory shops and Johnstons of Elgin, a knitwear and home interiors store founded in 1797.

can sometimes unearth a real gem. The helpful owner, Elizabeth Strong, will search for specific titles.

⊞ F3 ✉ 3a/4a Haddington Place, Leith Walk EH7 4AE ☎ 0131 556 5897 🚌 7, 10, 11, 12, 14, 16, 22, 25, 49

OPEN EYE GALLERY

openeyegallery.co.uk

This small gallery sells the work of Scottish painters, printmakers and sculptors past and present, as well as works by international masters from Picasso to Hockney.

⊞ D4 ✉ 34 Abercromby Place EH3 6QE ☎ 0131 557 1020 🚌 23, 27

PAPER TIGER

papertiger.co.uk

This popular shop sells an attractive range of fun and funky gifts, furnishings and household items.

⊞ A6 ✉ 6A/8 Stafford Street EH3 7AU ☎ 0131 226 2390 🚌 7, 104

THE RINGMAKER

theringmaker.co.uk

The place to go for a piece of bespoke jewelry designed in Scotland, this studio was founded in 1985 by artist and craftsman John Gilchrist. It uses diamonds, colored stones and precious metals to make not only rings but pendants, earrings, cufflinks and more.

⊞ C4 ✉ 46 Dundas Street EH3 6JN ☎ 0131 558 8800 🚌 23, 27

SCOTTISH NATIONAL GALLERY

nationalgalleries.org

The National Gallery shop has gifts, prints, jewelry, books and postcards. Lots of the designs are inspired by the gallery's collection.

⊞ D6 ✉ The Mound EH2 2EL ☎ 0131 624 6200 🚌 6, 23, 27, 41, 42, 67; free gallery bus

---

WILLIAM STREET

This cobbled street in Edinburgh's West End (at the junction of Stafford and Alva streets) has a concentration of small, specialized shops, including many independent designers of clothes and gifts. Have a mosey around the shops before taking a break in one of the old traditional pubs that help to retain the character of the street.

STEWART CHRISTIE & CO.

stewartchristie.com

Bespoke tailors for more than 200 years, Stewart Christie & Co. make garments on the premises. This family business provides country and formal clothing, including Scottish tweed jackets, moleskin trousers, Highland dress and tartan evening trousers.

⊞ B5 ✉ 63 Queen Street EH2 4NA ☎ 013 225 6639 🚌 24, 29, 42

VALVONA & CROLLA

valvonacrolla.co.uk

This beloved deli has barely changed since opening in 1934. Shelves are stacked with the finest Italian produce. Mozzarella is shipped from Naples, cured meats hang from the ceiling, and bread is baked on site daily.

⊞ F3 ✉ 19 Elm Row EH7 4AA ☎ 0131 55 6066 🚌 7, 10, 11, 12, 14, 16, 22, 25, 49

WAVERLEY MALL

waverleymall.com

You'll find the city's main post office, two currency exchange bureaux, a supermarket, food court and more than 20 stores in this multilevel mall (formerly Princes Mall) next to Waverle Station. Edinburgh's main tourist information office is at street level.

⊞ E5 ✉ Princes Street EH1 1BQ ☎ 0131 557 3759 🚌 All buses to Waverley Station

Entertainment and Nightlife

AMARONE

amaronerestaurant.co.uk

This stylish wine bar and restaurant in the heart of New Town has a good wine list and an Italian-inspired cocktail list.

⊞ D5 ⊠ 13 St. Andrew Square EH2 2AF
☎ 0131 523 1171 🕓 Mon–Fri 8am–10.30pm, Sat–Sun 10am–10.30pm 🚌 10, 11, 12, 16, 26
🚋 tram to St. Andrew Square

ASSEMBLY ROOMS

assemblyroomsedinburgh.co.uk

The elegant Georgian Assembly Rooms showcase mainstream Festival Fringe productions, in an impressive ballroom and music hall.

⊞ C5 ⊠ 54 George Street EH2 2LR ☎ 0131 220 4348 (box office) 🚌 10, 11, 12, 16, 41, 42

BAILIE BAR

thebailiebar.co.uk

Sample real ales at this New Town basement pub with an interesting triangular-shaped bar and low ceilings.

⊞ B3 ⊠ 2–4 St. Stephen Street EH3 5AL
☎ 0131 225 4673 🕓 Mon–Thu 11am–midnight, Fri–Sat 11am–1am, Sun 12.30–midnight 🚌 24, 29, 42

LGBTQ+

Edinburgh has a vibrant scene that revolves around Broughton Street, an area known as the Pink Triangle. Hotels, clubs, cafés and pubs cater to the gay community.
For pre-club drinks try The Basement (⊠ 10a–12a Broughton Street EH1 3RH ☎ 0131 557 0097; basement-bar-edinburgh.co.uk) or The Street (⊠ 2b Picardy Place EH1 3JT ☎ 0131 556 4272; thestreetbaredinburgh.co.uk). CC Blooms (⊠ 23 Greenside Place EH1 3AA ☎ 0131 556 9331) is a popular gay rendezvous during the day and turns into a lively club-style venue at night, open till 3am.

THE BARONY

thebarony.co.uk

This fine old bar and gastropub serves excellent dishes using Scottish produce and hosts live jazz on Saturday afternoons (3–5) and blues on Sunday evenings (7–9).

⊞ E3 ⊠ 81–85 Broughton Street EH1 3RJ
☎ 0131 556 9251 🕓 Daily 11am–1am 🚌 8

BOURBON BAR

bourbonedin.com

Opened in 2016, this venue combines a lounge bar with two separate club rooms that host club nights on Tuesday, Thursday, Friday and Saturday.

⊞ C5 ⊠ 24A Frederick Street EH2 2JR
☎ 0131 322 3190 🕓 Daily until 3am (1am Tue and Sun) 🚌 24, 29, 42

CAFÉ ROYAL

belhavenpubs.co.uk

Stop for a drink and admire the ornate ceiling, tiled portraits, stained glass and mahogany carvings here. The huge bar takes center stage.

⊞ E5 ⊠ 19 West Register Street EH2 2AA
☎ 0131 556 1884 🕓 Mon–Wed 11–11, Thu 11am–midnight, Fri–Sat 11am–1am, Sun 11am–midnight 🚌 1, 4, 19, 22, 25, 29, 34, 104, X15

EDINBURGH PLAYHOUSE

playhousetheatre.com

Big-budget musicals, dance shows and visiting rock bands make good use of this auditorium a short walk from the east end of Princes Street.

⊞ F4 ⊠ 18–22 Greenside Place EH1 3AA
☎ 0131 524 3333 🚌 1, 4, 5, 7, 8, 14, 19, 22, 25, 34, 45, 49

ESCAPE HUNT

escapehunt.com

For a night out with a difference, get yourself locked into a room with some

friends. To escape, you have to solve a range of baffling puzzles, but hurry—the clock is ticking!

C5 🖂 24 Castle Street EH2 3HT ☎ 0131 225 5522 🕙 Daily 10–10 🚌 25, 26, 44 and tram

LULU

luluedinburgh.co.uk

Tucked beneath the Tigerlily Hotel, Lulu is glamorous and fashionable—its weekly Buddha Fridays (featuring a huge ball pit and popcorn machines) and Lulu Saturdays are filled to capacity.

B5 🖂 125B George Street EH2 4JN ☎ 0131 225 5005 🕙 Thu–Mon 9pm–3am 🚌 10, 11, 12, 16, 41, 42

OPAL LOUNGE

opallounge.co.uk

This multipurpose basement space is stylish but casual. Here you'll find a diverse selection of events, from quiz nights and cocktail club evenings to electric groove yoga.

C5 🖂 51a George Street EH2 4HT ☎ 0131 226 2275 🕙 Mon–Thu 5pm–3am, Fri 4pm–3am, Sat–Sun noon–3am 🚌 10, 11, 12, 16, 41, 42

PUB LIFE

Edinburgh's bars, pubs, restaurants and cafés serve alcohol from 11am until 11pm (and often later, especially on Friday and Saturday nights). Some bars and restaurants allow diners to bring their own wine or beer (but not spirits), but may charge a corkage fee. Families with children are accepted in most restaurants and cafés, but kids are less welcome in pubs, especially in the evenings. The ban on smoking indoors accidentally created a sidewalk culture, and many bars and cafés now have tables outside where smokers can indulge.

OXFORD BAR

A must for fans of the Edinburgh literary scene, this undemonstrative real ale pu is frequented by many a local writer and artist. Perhaps the best-known of them all is crime writer Ian Rankin, who has made it the drinking hole of choice for his fictional Inspector Rebus.

B5 🖂 8 Young Street EH2 4JB ☎ 0131 539 7119 🕙 Mon–Thu noon–midnight, Fri–Sa 11am–1am, Sun 12.30–11 🚌 24, 29, 42

PANDA AND SONS

pandanadsons.com

Opened in 2013, this is an exotic cross between a Prohibition-era speakeasy and a vintage barber's shop. Sip a delicious cocktail created by the Panda team with an intriguing name such as Oaxacan Dad or Illicit Trade, or try one of their craft beers or wines.

B5 🖂 79 Queen Street EH2 4NF ☎ 013 220 0443 🕙 Mon–Fri 4pm–1am, Sat–Sun 3pm–1am 🚌 24, 29, 42

RABBLE

rabbleedinburgh.co.uk

Formerly known as Rick's, Rabble styles itself as a "rough-luxe taphouse and gri with rooms." Come for the glass-roofed garden, stay for the cocktails and unpas teurized craft beer straight from the venue's own copper tanks.

C5 🖂 55A Frederick Street EH2 1LH ☎ 0131 622 7800 🕙 Daily 7.30am–1am 🚌 24, 29, 42

ROSS OPEN AIR THEATRE

This is an impressive spot for a busy summer schedule of outdoor concerts and live events, right beneath Edinburgh Castle.

C6 🖂 West Princes Street Gardens EH2 2HG ☎ 0131 228 8616 🚌 1, 3, 4, 22, 24, 2 30, 31, 33, 34, 37, 41, 44, X5, X25, X31, X37, X

SHANGHAI

shanghaiclub.co.uk

In the basement of Le Monde hotel, this state-of-the-art club with an oriental touch prides itself on being Edinburgh's top late-night venue.

🔲 D5 ✉ 16 George Street EH2 2PF ☎ 0131 270 3900 🕐 Daily 10pm–3am 🚌 10, 11, 12, 16, 41, 42

THE STAND

thestand.co.uk

This basement venue is pivotal to the Scottish stand-up comedy circuit. It's a key venue during the Edinburgh Fringe, and the rest of the year presents a mixture of established and new talent.

🔲 E4 ✉ 5 York Place EH1 3EB ☎ 0131 558 7272 🕐 Show times vary 🚌 10, 11, 12, 16, 26, 44

SUPERCUBE

supercube.biz

Who doesn't love a good old sing-along? Here you and your friends get your own wireless mics, songbooks packed with over 50,000 tracks and state-of-the-art sound system. Everyone's karaoke skills are oiled by drinks and snacks brought by attentive staff.

🔲 C5 ✉ 58A George Street EH2 2LR ☎ 0131 226 4218 🕐 Mon–Thu 5pm–3am, Fri 2pm–3am, Sat–Sun noon–3am 🚌 10, 11, 12, 16, 41, 42

NEW TOWN ENTERTAINMENT AND NIGHTLIFE/WHERE TO EAT

Where to Eat

PRICES

Prices are approximate, based on a 3-course meal for one person.

£££ over £25
££ £15–£25
£ under £15

BELL'S DINER (£–££)

bellsdineredinburgh.co.uk

Bell's hasn't changed its formula for more than 40 years. This little gem has been serving classic burgers and steaks smothered with your own choice of sauce in the heart of bohemian Stockbridge since the 1970s. It may not be the most trendy but it's easy to see why it has such a loyal local following.

🔲 B3 ✉ 7 St. Stephen Street EH3 5AN ☎ 0131 225 8116 🕐 Mon 5–9, Tue–Fri 5–10, Sat 12.20–10, Sun 4–9 🚌 24, 29, 42

LE CAFÉ ST. HONORÉ (£££)

cafesthonore.com

Enjoy intimate, relaxed dining in a French-style restaurant serving a fine blend of Scottish and French dishes.

🔲 C5 ✉ 34 NW Thistle Street Lane EH2 1EA ☎ 0131 226 2211 🕐 Daily noon–2, 5.30–10 🚌 6, 23, 27, 67

CONTINI RISTORANTE (£££)

contini.com

Family-run Contini occupies its own niche in the panoply of Edinburgh's

EATING ITALIAN

Large numbers of Italians emigrated to Scotland in the early 20th century, bringing with them their own culinary influences. Hence you will find many good Italian restaurants, mostly in Edinburgh's West End.

Italian restaurants, with classic pasta dishes given a modern spin and a dizzying array of menus, including one for vegans and those on a low-gluten diet.

➕ C5 ✉ 103 George Street EH2 3ES
☎ 0131 225 1550 🕐 Mon–Fri 8am–10.30pm, Sat 10am–10.30pm, Sun 10–10 🚌 10, 11, 12, 16, 41, 42

CORO THE CHOCOLATE CAFÉ (£–££)

corochocolate.co.uk

Coro's mission statement is "to give you your chocolate fix," so whether you like your particular hit with crepes, waffles or pancakes, or as a fondue with fresh fruit, you'll be well served here. You can even create your own dessert.

➕ C5 ✉ 13 Frederick Street EH2 2EY
☎ 0131 225 4477 🕐 Daily 10–10 🚌 24, 29, 42

DOME (£££)

thedomeedinburgh.com

The Dome is a classy venue in a converted bank with a magnificent glass dome as the focal point. They describe

---

their style as a "celebration of simple and traditional Scottish favorites." There also a tearoom serving delicate sandwiches and sumptuous pastries.

➕ D5 ✉ 14 George Street EH2 2PF
☎ 0131 624 8624 🕐 Daily 10–late
🚌 10, 11, 12, 16, 41, 42

EDEN'S KITCHEN (££)

edens-kitchen.com

This bistro serves meze and main courses, pasta, pizza and burgers, and offers an above-average kids' menu. Eden's Kitchen has a bring-your-own alcohol policy and, conveniently, there's a good liquor store opposite.

➕ E3 ✉ 32c Broughton Street EH1 3SB
☎ 0131 556 6588 🕐 Mon–Thu noon–10.30, Fri–Sat noon–11 🚌 Tram to York Place

EDUCATED FLEA (£££)

educatedflea.co.uk

Educated Flea serves Asian-fusion dishes such as truffle-scented braised beef featherblade or baked romano peppers with baharat-spiced rice, plus an array of Scottish-influenced starters and main courses.

➕ E3 ✉ 32b Broughton Street EH1 3SB
☎ 0131 556 8092 🕐 Mon noon–2.30, 5–9, Tue–Fri noon–2.30, 5–10, Sat 10–10, Sun 10–9 🚌 Tram to York Place

GALLERY RESTAURANT AT THE GUILDFORD ARMS (£££)

guildfordarms.com

Built in 1896 at the height of the temperance movement and owned by the same family ever since, the Guildford Arms is a beautiful pub with an unusual gallery that serves as a lofty restaurant. Enjoy your lunchtime ciabatt sandwich or evening haggis or veggie Wellington in surroundings of etched glass and Victorian cornicing.

DINE WITH A VIEW

For fine food and spectacular views try the Forth Floor Restaurant at Harvey Nichols (✉ 30–34 St. Andrew Square EH2 2AD ☎ 0131 524 8350; harveynichols.com), which has a balcony and floor-to-ceiling windows providing striking views of the Castle in one direction and the Firth of Forth in the other. The Tower Restaurant (▷ 44) is on the fifth floor of the National Museum of Scotland (▷ 27) and offers superb views of the Castle, the incredible skyline of the Royal Mile and over Old Town. This is rooftop dining at its best. The Starbank Inn (▷ 106) looks out over the Firth of Forth to Fife.

➕ E5 ✉ 1 West Register Street EH2 2AA
☎ 0131 556 4312 ⏰ Sun–Wed 11–11, Thu–Sat 11am–midnight 🚌 1, 4, 19, 22, 25, 29, 34, 104, 113, X15, X25, X26, X44

LA GARRIGUE (£££)

lagarrigue.co.uk

A showcase for food from the Languedoc region in France, Garrigue serves hearty Gallic cooking with finesse, and the wines and cheeses are also from the region. With the dominant blue paint and the wooden furniture, there is a strong Mediterranean feel.

➕ F6 ✉ 31 Jeffrey Street EH1 1DH ☎ 0131 557 3032 ⏰ Daily 12–2.30, 6–9.30 🚌 35 and all buses to Waverley Station

HENDERSON'S VEGAN RESTAURANT (££–£££)

hendersonsofedinburgh.co.uk

An Edinburgh institution, the former Henderson's Bistro serves dishes made with super-fresh ingredients, organic where possible, in a light, pleasant environment. Try the celeriac gnocchi or a jackfruit, tomato and coconut stew.

➕ D5 ✉ 25c Thistle Street EH2 1DX ☎ 0131 225 2605 ⏰ Daily noon–9 🚌 6, 13, 27, 67

HOLY COW (£)

Holy Cow's menu is not only 100 percent vegan but favors fairtrade and organic ingredients as well. Choose from Muu burgers, Holy Sandwiches, super-green salads and other wholesome fare.

➕ E4 ✉ 34 Elder Street EH1 3DX ⏰ Sun–Fri 10–10, Sat 9am–10pm 🚌 10, 11, 12, 16, 26, 34 and tram

HOWIES (££)

howies.uk.com

In a delightful 200-year-old Georgian building, this restaurant offers fresh Scottish produce such as baked salmon or steak, or the less traditional charred parsnip and chickpea fritter, all imaginatively served. From Sunday to Thursday you can bring your own wine.

➕ F5 ✉ 29 Waterloo Place EH1 3BQ ☎ 0131 556 5766 ⏰ Mon–Fri noon–2.30, 5.30–10, Sat–Sun noon–3, 5.30–10 🚌 X5, X7, X15, X17, X18, X25, X27, X28, X44

KWEILIN (£££)

kweilin.net

Enjoy beautifully cooked traditional Cantonese cuisine in Chinese-style surroundings. The menu offers a great selection, and there is an excellent wine list. There's another branch serving Chinese/Japanese cuisine at 26–30 Potterrow in Old Town.

➕ C4 ✉ 19–21 Dundas Street EH3 6QG ☎ 0131 557 1875 ⏰ Tue–Thu 12–2, 5.30–10.30, Fri–Sat 12–2, 5.30–11 🚌 23, 27

THE MAGNUM (£–£££)

themagnumrestaurant.co.uk

Is it a bistro? A restaurant? A pub? A wine bar? The folk at Magnum like to keep people guessing. Head chef Paul Dow uses fresh local produce in season to create dishes such as the classic Cullen skink (smoked haddock soup) and rather less traditional pumpkin and sage ravioli.

➕ D4 ✉ 1 Albany Street EH1 3PY ☎ 0131 557 4366 ⏰ Mon–Thu noon–2.30, 5.30–10, Fri–Sun noon–10 🚌 10, 11, 12, 16, 26, 44

MIRO'S (£££)

miroscantinamexicana.com

This small restaurant has been giving Edinburghers a flavor of Mexico for nearly 30 years. Serving a mixture of home-cooked traditional dishes and more contemporary Mexican fare, they use fresh local produce and ingredients

sourced from Mexico for that authentic *sabor mexicano*.

+ B5 ⊠ 184 Rose Street EH2 4BA ☎ 0131 225 4376 🕓 Daily noon–10.30 🚌 24, X31, X33, X37 and tram

MUSSEL INN (£££)

mussel-inn.com

The tastiest shellfish, scallops and oysters are delivered fresh from the Scottish sea lochs to this bustling eatery in the heart of New Town.

+ C5 ⊠ 61–65 Rose Street EH2 2NH ☎ 0131 225 5979 🕓 Mon–Thu noon–3, 5.30–10, Fri–Sat noon–10, Sun 12.30–10 🚌 25, 26, 44 and tram

NOVAPIZZA (£££)

novapizza.co.uk

This popular vegan and vegetarian Italian restaurant offers a wide range of beautifully presented pizzas, though you might also be tempted by some of their other creative dishes, suchs as *penne alla vodka* and *seitan alla pizzaiola*.

+ C4 ⊠ 42 Howe Street EH3 6TH ☎ 0131 237 5695 🕓 Mon, Wed 3.30–9.30, Thu–Sun 12.30–9.30 🚌 24, 29, 42

OLIVE BRANCH (££)

theolivebranchscotland.co.uk

A modern decor of wooden floors, bare brick walls and black leather, wicker and velour seating is the setting for innovative seasonal dishes with a Mediterranean slant, and good old-fashioned comfort food. Large windows enable serious people-watching.

+ E3 ⊠ 91 Broughton Street EH1 3RX ☎ 0131 557 8589 🕓 Daily 10–10

LA P'TITE FOLIE (££)

laptitefolie.co.uk

The French cuisine more than measures up to the outstanding Tudor building

housing this cheerful eatery, where the tables are rather close together. The owner has opened a wine bar—Le Di-Vin—in the same building.

+ A5 ⊠ Tudor House, 9 Randolph Place EH3 7TE ☎ 0131 225 8678 🕓 Mon–Thu noon–3 6–10, Fri–Sat noon–3, 6–11 🚌 19, 36, 41, 43, 47, 103, 113, X5, X7, X37, X43, X47

SMOKE STACK (££)

smokestack.org.uk

Fabulous steaks, huge portions and a great location make Smoke Stack popular. It's not fancy, but the prices are reasonable and the food excellent.

+ E3 ⊠ 53–55 Broughton Street EH1 3RJ ☎ 0131 556 6032 🕓 Daily 9am–10pm 🚌 8

VINCAFFÈ (££)

valvonacrolla.co.uk

The owners of Scotland's oldest delicatessen, Valvona & Crolla (▷ 80), opened this café/wine bar to create a Continental-style meeting place. Their own ingredients are used to create tasty Italian food, washed down by a glass of wine from their range.

+ E4 ⊠ Jenners, 47–48 Princes Street EH2 2YJ ☎ 0131 260 2386 🕓 Mon–Sat 7.30am–late, Sun 10am–late 🚌 All buses to Waverley Station

VOODOO ROOMS (££–£££)

thevoodoorooms.com

The sophisticated wood-paneled black and gold Voodoo Rooms boast a bar holding 60 different tequilas and a menu offering Duart salmon and cauliflower risotto with chocolate jelly. The venue has live music every night from Wednesday to Saturday.

+ E5 ⊠ 19A West Register Street EH2 2AA ☎ 0131 556 7060 🕓 Mon–Thu 4pm–1am, Fri–Sun noon–1am 🚌 1, 4, 19, 22, 29, 34, 10 113, X15, X25, X26, X44

Farther Afield

There's plenty to see right on the doorstep of the city and the transportation is good. From the award-winning RZSS Edinburgh Zoo to the Royal Yacht *Britannia* at Leith, the attractions in this chapter make for great days out.

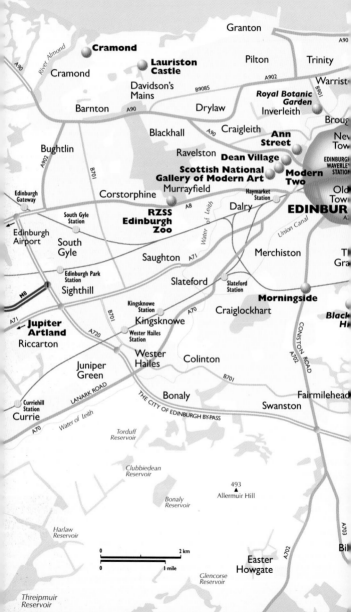

Cramond Island

Drum Sands

Granton

A90

Cramond

Pilton

Trinity

Cramond

Lauriston Castle

Warrist

River Almond

A90

Davidson's Mains

B9085

A902

Royal Botanic Garden

B901

Barnton

A90

Drylaw

Inverleith

Broug

Blackhall

A90

Craigleith

Ann Street

New Tow

Bughtlin

A902

B701

Ravelston

Dean Village

EDINBURGH WAVERLEY STATION

Modern Two

Edinburgh Gateway

Corstorphine

Scottish National Gallery of Modern Art

Murrayfield

A8

Old Tow

EDINBUR

South Gyle Station

RZSS Edinburgh Zoo

Haymarket Station

Dalry

A

Water of Leith

Union Canal

T Gra

Edinburgh Airport

South Gyle

Saughton

A71

Merchiston

Edinburgh Park Station

Sighthill

Slateford

Slateford Station

M8

Kingsknowe Station

B701

Kingsknowe

A70

Craiglockhart

Morningside

A71

Jupiter Artland

A720

Wester Hailes Station

Black H

Riccarton

Wester Hailes

Colinton

CONISTON ROAD

A702

Juniper Green

LANARK ROAD

B701

Bonaly

Fairmilehead

Curriehill Station

THE CITY OF EDINBURGH BY-PASS

Swanston

Currie

A70

Water of Leith

Torduff Reservoir

Clubbiedean Reservoir

493 ▲ Allermuir Hill

Bonaly Reservoir

Harlaw Reservoir

A703

0 ———————— 2 km
0 ———————— 1 mile

Easter Howgate

A702

Bi

Glencorse Reservoir

Threipmuir Reservoir

Firth of Forth

Royal Yacht
Britannia

Leith

A199

A900

Meadowbank

A1140

B6415

Portobello

Niddrie
dykes

Holyrood Park
251
Arthur's Seat

Northfield

A1

Fisherrow Sands

Duddingston

Bingham

Brunstane
Station

Brunstane

Fisherrow

Musselburgh

Musselburgh
Station

A7

Prestonfield

A6095

Newcraighall
Station

Stoneybank

Craigmillar

**Craigmillar
Castle**

The
Inch

A6106

MILLERHILL ROAD

Shawfair
Station

A701

Moredun

A7

Danderhall

GILMERTON ROAD

A771

Liberton

OLD DALKEITH ROAD

A720

THE CITY OF EDINBURGH BY-PASS

*Dalkeith
Park*

Gracemount

A772

Dalkeith

Loanhead

A768

A768

River North Esk

Lasswade

A7

Eskbank
Station

River South Esk

Bonnyrigg

A6094

B703

Newtongrange

B6392

B704

Roslin

Craigmillar Castle

TOP 25

HIGHLIGHTS

- Views
- Substantial ruins
- Queen Mary's Room
- Former chapel and dovecote

TIP

- Don't be put off by the journey to the castle through some of Edinburgh's less admired housing developments— it's worth the effort.

The ruins of one of Scotland's most impressive 15th-century tower houses are particularly pleasant to visit when the hustle and bustle of Edinburgh becomes too much.

Splendid remains Craigmillar lies 4km (2.5 miles) southeast of the heart of the city and is often overlooked because of the more famous Edinburgh Castle. At its core is a well-preserved early 15th-century L-plan tower house with walls up to 2.7m (9ft) thick, constructed on the site of an older fortification by Sir George Preston. The main defensive features—massive doors, a spiral turnpike stair (connecting three floors), narrow passage-ways and two outer walls to fend off English attackers—make it a great place to explore.

Surprisingly rural considering its proximity to the city, Craigmillar Castle makes a relaxing afternoon out

Fit for a queen Mary, Queen of Scots fled here on several occasions when the pressures of life at Holyrood became too great, notably after the murder of her secretary and darling David Rizzio in 1566, and the tiny chamber where she slept bears her name. It is said that during this stay conspirators agreed to the "Craigmillar Bond," the plot to kill Lord Darnley, Mary's unscrupulous and unpopular husband.

Falling into ruin Craigmillar was bought from the Prestons by Sir John Gilmour in 1660 to convert into a fashionable residence. The family, however, decided to move to Inch House at Gilmerton instead and Craigmillar was abandoned. Overgrown and ruinous, it was acquired by the state in 1946, and is now in the hands of Historic Environment Scotland.

THE BASICS

historicenvironment.scot

✚ See map ▷ 89

✉ Craigmillar Castle Road EH16 4SY

☎ 0131 661 4445

🕐 Apr–Sep daily 9.30–5.30; Oct daily 10–4; Nov–Mar Sat–Wed 9.30–4.30

🚌 2, 14, 30

♿ Poor, but access to visitor area

💷 Moderate

Leith

HIGHLIGHTS

- The Shore
- Ocean Terminal
- Water of Leith visitor center
- Royal Yacht *Britannia*

TIP

- Choose a dry and, if possible, sunny day to visit Leith to get the most from the coastal location.

Edinburgh's seaport, amalgamated with the city in 1920, has been a dock area since the 14th century. Following a decline in shipbuilding, it has been regenerated to attract tourism.

New role Leith was for many years a prosperous town in its own right. As the shipbuilding industry began to wane in the 20th century the town went into decline, but it has come up in the world again and now it buzzes with fashionable eating places. The area known as The Shore, along the waterfront, is filled with flourishing bars and restaurants. Warehouses, once full of wine and whisky, have been converted into smart accommodations. Where Tower Street meets The Shore, look for the Signal Tower, built in 1685–86 as a windmill.

Clockwise from left: Fishers Leith restaurant and bar; take a cruise out from the waterside at Leith; working boats in Leith docks; new apartments at Leith are popular, especially with young city workers

Edinburgh's river, the Water of Leith, flows through the middle of the town and the visitor center tells more about its heritage.

Historic Leith The town has witnessed its share of history—Mary, Queen of Scots landed here from France in 1561 and reputedly stayed at Andro Lamb's House, in Water Street. King James II banned golf from Leith Links as it interfered with archery practice. The original 13 rules of golf were drawn up here in 1744, but in 1907 the dunes were flattened to create a public park and golf was banished once more.

Modern town For visitors, the Royal Yacht *Britannia* (▷ 95) is the main draw, as well as the Ocean Terminal Centre, one of Europe's largest shopping and leisure complexes.

THE BASICS

- ✚ See map ▷ 89
- ✉ Leith
- 🚌 1, 11, 16, 22, 34, 35, 36, Skylink 200
- 🛈 VisitScotland, 94 Ocean Drive EH6 6JH
- ☎ 0131 472 2222

Royal Botanic Garden

The entrance gate to the gardens (left) and an orchid from the collection (right)

THE BASICS

rbge.org.uk
🚩 B1
✉ 20a Inverleith Row
EH3 5LR
☎ 0131 248 2909
🕐 Mar–Sep daily 10–6;
Feb, Oct daily 10–5;
Nov–Jan daily 10–4
🍴 Gateway Restaurant
and Terrace Café
🚌 8, 23, 27
♿ Good
💷 Entry to garden free;
glasshouses moderate;
tours moderate
❓ Tours lasting around
60 minutes leave the John
Hope Gateway Reception
at 11 and 2, Apr–Oct

HIGHLIGHTS

● Rock Garden
● Glasshouses
● Tropical Aquatic House
● Chinese Hillside
● Scottish Heath Garden
● The gates
● Orchid and Cycad House
● Woodland Garden

Known locally as The Botanics, these gardens boast some 15,500 species, one of the largest collections of living plants in the world. It's possibly Edinburgh's finest recreational asset.

City greenery Occupying this site since 1823, the gardens cover more than 28ha (69 acres) of beautifully landscaped and wooded grounds to the north of the city, forming an immaculately maintained green oasis. You can walk to the garden from Princes Street via Stockbridge, though you may wish to take the bus back up the hill afterward.

Inside or out? There are 10 glasshouses to explore, offering a perfect haven on cold days. They include an amazingly tall palm house dating back to 1834, and the Plant and People House, with its giant waterlilies and an underwater view of fish swimming through the lily roots. Outside, the plants of the Chinese Hillside and the Scottish Heath Garden are particularly interesting, and in summer the herbaceous borders are breathtaking. Check out the rhododendron collection and the Rock Garden, which displays some 5,000 species and is best seen in May. The highest point of the garden has a fine view of the city.

Striking design The West Gate, or Carriage Gate, is the main entrance, but don't miss the stunning inner east side gates, designed by local architect Ben Tindall in 1996.

The Royal Yacht
Britannia (left) has a
full-size lounge within
its hull (right)

Royal Yacht *Britannia*

This former royal yacht is one of the world's most famous ships, now permanently moored in Edinburgh's historic Port of Leith. It is 83rd in a long line of royal yachts stretching back to 1660.

New role *Britannia* was decommissioned in 1997 after a cut in government funds. It had carried the Queen and her family on 968 official voyages all over the world since its launch at Clydebank in 1953.

Vital statistics For 40 years, *Britannia* served the royal family, sailing more than 1 million miles to become one of the most famous ships in the world. A compact yacht, it is just 125.6m (412ft) long. It carried a crew of 240, including a Royal Marine band and an additional 45 household staff when the royal family were on board. A self-guided tour using handsets takes you around the yacht itself. *Britannia* still retains the fittings and furnishings of her working days, which gives an intimate insight into the royals away from usual palace protocol.

Royal and naval precision Check out the apartments adorned with hundreds of original items from the royal collection. The grandest room is the State Dining Room, and the most elegant the Drawing Room. Imagine the royal family relaxing in the Sun Lounge and view the modest sleeping quarters. Everything on board is shipshape, from the Engine Room to the fully equipped Sick Bay.

THE BASICS

royalyachtbritannia.co.uk
☐ See map ▷ 89
✉ Ocean Terminal, Leith
EH6 6JJ
☎ 0131 555 5566
🕐 Apr–Oct daily
9.30–4.30; Nov–Mar daily
10–3.30
🍴 Royal Deck Tea Room
🚌 11, 22, 34, 35, 36,
Skylink 200
♿ Excellent
💷 Expensive
❓ Reservations strongly
advised in high season

HIGHLIGHTS

● Royal Apartments
● Drawing Room
● State Dining Room
● Sun Lounge
● Royal Bedrooms
● Sick Bay and Operating
Theatre
● Engine Room
● The Bridge

FARTHER AFIELD TOP 25

RZSS Edinburgh Zoo

HIGHLIGHTS

● Giant and red pandas
● Walkthrough exhibits
● Tiger Tracks enclosure
● Penguins Rock
● Budongo Trail
● Koala Territory

TIP

● To see the giant pandas you need a separate timed ticket. This is free but spaces are limited so book in advance.

Giant pandas Tian Tian and Yang Guang are the star attractions at RZSS Edinburg Zoo, which promotes conservation while offering a great day out.

Conservation, education and fun RZSS Edinburgh Zoo is a world leader in breeding endangered species. It also campaigns to protect wildlife worldwide, while demonstrating how a visitor attraction can modernize to survive. Located at Corstorphine, 5km (3 miles) west of the city center, the zoo covers 33ha (82 acres) of wooded hillside and is home to around 1,000 animals.

Natural habitats New-generation exhibits allow visitors to encounter pelicans, wallabies and lemurs in walk-through exhibits, and get

Clockwise from far left: On lookout, a meerkat stands guard at Edinburgh Zoo; Ruaridh the red panda was born in 2019; one of the zoo's two giant pandas; 18th-century Mansion House, at the heart of the zoo, is a popular venue for functions; gentoo penguins on parade

...ose to big cats through a glass tunnel that ...uns through the Tiger Tracks enclosure. ...here's also an aerial walkway across rolling ...llocks, and the Budongo Trail, where you ...an see chimpanzees in a unique interactive ...door/outdoor enclosure.

...andas and penguins Tian Tian (female) and ...ang Guang (male), on loan from China, are ...e only giant pandas in Britain. Pandas are ...litary creatures, so they are kept in separate ...closures. The red pandas (an only distantly ...lated species) are also very popular, especially ...e baby born in 2019. Penguins Rock is ...urope's largest penguin pool, complete ...ith waterfall, and the Penguin Parade, when ...enguins waddle around the enclosure with ...eir keepers, is a daily highlight.

THE BASICS

edinburghzoo.org.uk
+ See map ▷ 88
✉ Corstorphine Road EH12 6TS
☎ 0131 334 9171
🕐 Apr–Sep daily 10–6; Oct, Mar daily 10–5; Nov–Feb daily 10–4
🍽 Restaurant, café, kiosks and picnic areas
🚌 12, 26, 31, X17, X18, Airlink 100
♿ Very good
💷 Expensive

Scottish National Gallery of Modern Art

TOP **25**

Outside the gallery; Le Coureur (The Runner), by Germaine Richier

THE BASICS

nationalgalleries.org

➕ See map ▷ 88

✉ 75 Belford Road EH4 3DR

☎ 0131 624 6200

🕐 Daily 10–5

🍴 Café Modern One, Palozzi's Kitchen

🚌 Free bus links all three national galleries

🚆 Edinburgh Haymarket

♿ Very good

💷 Free, but may be charges for temporary exhibitions

HIGHLIGHTS

● Works by the Scottish Colourists, including those by John Duncan Fergusson
● Major works by Picasso, Matisse and Lichtenstein
● Sculptures by Henry Moore and Barbara Hepworth
● Works by contemporary artists, including Damien Hirst and Rachel Whiteread
● Eduardo Paolozzi's studio

The gallery opened at this parkland site in 1984, providing an ideal setting for the work of those who have been in the forefront of modern art: Matisse, Picasso, Hirst. You'll find them all here.

Setting the scene The first thing you see as you arrive at the main gallery is a sweeping, living sculpture of grassy terraces and semi-circular ponds, an installation called *Landform UEDA* by Charles Jencks. After such a grand introduction, the rest of the gallery seems quite small, but that belies its enviable collection of modern art from around the world. It is housed in a former school.

On display Regularly changing exhibitions occupy the first floor, with a varied display from the gallery's collection on the second floor. Look for works by Picasso, Braque and Matisse, Hepworth and Gabo. The work of the early 20th-century group of painters known as the Scottish Colourists is particularly striking, with canvases by Samuel John Peploe (1871–1935), John Duncan Fergusson (1874–1961) and F.C.B. Cadell (1883–1937). Also of interest are Fergusson's dramatic *Portrait of Anne Estelle Rice* (c.1908), the vibrancy of Cadell's *The Blue Fan* (c.1922) and Peploe's later, more fragmentary work, such as *Iona Landscape, Rocks* (c.1927).

More art Stroll across the road to Modern Two (▷ 100), an outstation of the gallery.

ANN STREET

The estate built in 1814 by artist Sir Henry Raeburn in memory of his wife, Ann, is one of Edinburgh's most exclusive addresses. The houses combine classic splendor with cottagey charm.

✚ A4 ✉ Ann Street 🚌 24, 29, 42

BLACKFORD HILL

oe.ac.uk

Just 3km (2 miles) south of the city center is one of Edinburgh's seven hills. It is home to the Royal Observatory, Edinburgh, which moved here from Calton Hill in 1895. The visitor area is open only for group visits and irregular events. There are occasional evening viewing sessions and talks (book in advance; tel 0131 668 8404).

✚ See map ▷ 88 ✉ Blackford 🚌 38, 41 ♿ Few

CRAMOND

cramondheritage.org.uk

There are Roman remains, 16th-century houses, a fine church, an old inn and some elegant Victorian villas to hold your attention in this attractive suburb on the shores of the Firth of Forth. The Cramond Heritage Trust has a permanent exhibition in the Maltings, exploring the history of the village. Take one of the good walks around the area or visit Lauriston Castle (▷ 100), nearby.

✚ See map ▷ 88 ✉ Cramond
🕐 Maltings: Apr–Sep Sat–Sun 2–5; every afternoon during Festival 🚌 41

DEAN VILLAGE

The northern limit of New Town is marked by Thomas Telford's 1831 Dean Bridge. It spans a steep gorge created by the Water of Leith. The workers' cottages, warehouses and mill buildings have been restored and Dean has become a desirable residential area. The cemetery is the resting place of many well-known locals, including the New Town architect William Playfair.

✚ See map ▷ 88 ✉ Dean 🚌 19, 37, 41, 43, 47, 113

FARTHER AFIELD MORE TO SEE

Take in the view over Edinburgh from Blackford Hill

Rows of boats at Cramond waterside

JUPITER ARTLAND

jupiterartland.org

This cutting-edge collection of contemporary landscape art and installations includes works by Phyllida Barlow, Andy Goldsworthy and Ian Hamilton Finlay, scattered around a 40ha (100-acre) estate surrounding Bonnington House.

➕ See map ▷ 88 ✉ Bonnington House Steadings, Wilkiestone EH27 8BY ☎ 01506 889 900 🕙 Mid-May to Sep daily 10–5 🚌 X27 🎫 Moderate

LAURISTON CASTLE

edinburghmuseums.org.uk

This "castle" is the epitome of Edwardian comfort and style, a gabled and turreted mansion overlooking the Firth of Forth near Cramond. Starting out as a simple tower house, it was renovated and extended several times and left to the City of Edinburgh in 1926 by William Robert Reid.

➕ See map ▷ 88 ✉ 2 Cramond Road South, Davidson's Mains EH4 6AD ☎ 0131 336 2060 🕙 Apr–Oct Mon–Thu tours at

2, Sat–Sun tours 2, 2.30 and 3.30; Nov–Mar Sat–Sun at 2 and 3. Grounds daily Apr–Sep 8–8; Oct–Mar daily 8–5 🚌 21, 41 ♿ Poor 🎫 Castle: moderate. Grounds: free

MODERN TWO

Part of the Gallery of Modern Art (▷ 98), this annex is housed in a former orphanage and displays an excellent collection based around the work of Dada and the Surrealists, and the Scottish sculptor Eduardo Paolozzi (1924–2005).

➕ See map ▷ 88 ✉ 73 Belford Road EH4 3DR ☎ 0131 624 6200 🕙 Daily 10–5 🚌 Free gallery bus 🚉 Edinburgh Haymarket ♿ Very good 🎫 Free

MORNINGSIDE

Immortalized in the accent of novelist Muriel Spark's Jean Brodie, this quiet, leafy suburb still houses the wealthy of the city in elegant Victorian villas. Stroll round its pleasant streets for civilized shopping and afternoon tea.

➕ See map ▷ 88 ✉ Morningside 🚌 5, 11, 15, 16, 23, 36, X15

Cells of Life by landscape architect Charles Jencks at Jupiter Artland

Excursions

MURRAYFIELD

Developed around the 18th-century Murrayfield House, this western suburb is a pleasant district and popular with city commuters. Scottish rugby has made its home here and Murrayfield hosts games during the Six Nations championships. The stadium was built by the Scottish Football Union and opened in 1925. A £70 million redevelopment gave it a new look and the ground was reopened by the Princess Royal in 1994. Murrayfield once held the world record for the largest attendance at a rugby game. This was for the match when Scotland played Wales in the Five Nations (as it was then) in 1975, drawing an enormous crowd of just over 104,000. Scotland won 12–10, inflicting Wales' only defeat of the tournament. The stadium's current seating capacity is 67,000.

THE BASICS

Distance: 2km (1.5 miles)
Journey time:
20 minutes
Murrayfield Stadium
✉ Corstorphine Road EH12 5PJ
☎ 0131 346 5000; scottishrugby.org
♿ Good
🚌 12, 26, 31, X17, X18, Airlink 100
❓ Stadium tours available Mon–Sat at 11 (also 2.30 Thu–Sat); expensive

NORTH BERWICK

Once a small fishing port, North Berwick, on the south side of the Firth of Forth to the east of Edinburgh, has developed into a lively holiday resort. Pleasure craft crowd the little port and its splendid Victorian and Edwardian architecture suggests prosperity. Golf is the number one attraction of the area dubbed the North Berwick Golf Coast and has been played here since the 17th century. The Scottish Seabird Centre uses the latest technology to take pictures of seabirds nesting on the nearby cliffs and islands, and there are interactive and multimedia displays to interest all the family, as well as boat trips from April to October. Behind the town is the cone of the North Berwick Law, a 187m-high (613ft) volcanic plug, which rewards hikers with fine views from the top over the Fife coastline to the Forth Road Bridge and Edinburgh Castle.

THE BASICS

Distance: 40km (25 miles)
Journey time:
30 minutes
🚆 From Waverley
ℹ Quality Street
☎ 01620 892197
Scottish Seabird Centre
✉ The Harbour, North Berwick EH39 4SS
☎ 01620 890202; seabird.org
🕐 Apr–Aug daily 10–6; Feb–Mar, Sep–Oct daily 10–5; Nov–Dec daily 10–4, Jan daily 11–4
💷 Expensive

THE BASICS

rosslynchapel.com
Distance: 11km (7 miles)
Journey time: 1 hour
✉ Roslin EH25 9PU
☎ 0131 440 2159
🕐 Jun–Aug Mon–Sat
9.30–6, Sun noon–4.45;
Sep–May Mon–Sat 9.30–5,
Sun noon–4.45
♿ Moderate
🚌 37, 140

ROSSLYN CHAPEL

In a tiny mining village south of Edinburgh, perched above Roslin Glen, this is one of the most mysterious buildings in Scotland. Founded in 1446 by William St. Clair, 3rd Earl of Orkney, the church was to be a large cruciform structure, but only the choir was completed, along with sections of the east transept walls. It is linked with the Knights Templar and other secretive societies, and is even believed by some to be the hiding place of the Holy Grail. The chapel found increased fame through its connection with the best-selling 2003 novel *The Da Vinci Code* by Dan Brown and was a location in the movie adaptation. Inside is a fine example of medieval stone-carving. The chapel remains in the hands of the St. Clair family and is still a place of worship.

THE BASICS

Distance: 26km
(16 miles)
Journey time: 1 hour
🚆 From Waverley to
Dalmeny station
🚌 43
ℹ Forth Bridges Tourist
Information Centre,
Queensferry Lodge
Hotel, North Queensferry
☎ 01383 417759
Hopetoun House
✉ South Queensferry
EH30 9RW ☎ 0131
331 2451; hopetoun.
co.uk 🕐 Easter–Sep daily
10.30–5 ♿ Expensive.
Grounds only: inexpensive

SOUTH QUEENSFERRY

From the 11th century until 1964, a ferry operated across the Firth of Forth from South Queensferry; then the road suspension bridge opened. The distinctive red, cantilevered rail bridge built in the late 19th century has become an icon of Scotland and was declared a Unesco World Heritage Site in 2015. Only a short ride outside Edinburgh, this little royal burgh with its attractive clock tower (right) is a great place to come to admire the three Forth bridges (the Queensferry Crossing opened in 2017) on a summer's evening. To the west, Hopetoun House—which can only be reached easily by car—is a spectacular 18th-century mansion built by William Bruce and William Adam. Home to the Marquis of Linlithgow, it is full of fine paintings, original furniture, tapestries and elaborate rococo detail. From the grounds there are more great views of the Forth bridges.

JUBILEE CLOCK 1887

Shopping

GOLDEN HARE BOOKS

goldenharebooks.com

This independent bookstore stocks a strong portfolio of intelligent fiction and nonfiction, beautifully illustrated editions, books for children and work by Edinburgh-based novelists and poets.

➕ Off map ✉ 68 Stephen Street EH3 5AQ ☎ 0131 225 7755 🚌 24, 29, 42

HALIBUT AND HERRING

halibutandherring.co.uk

If you're looking for a gift that's different, head to this small shop in the attractive Bruntsfield district. There's a big selection of bathtime products, as well as funky jewelry, unorthodox homeware, cute toys and unusual cards.

➕ B9 ✉ 108 Bruntsfield Place EH10 4ES ☎ 0131 229 2669 🚌 11, 16, 23, 36, 45, X15

KINLOCH ANDERSON

kinlochanderson.com

While browsing for kilts, tartan trousers, jackets, skirts and accessories, you can learn more about the history of tartan from the experts on Highland dress since 1868.

➕ Off map ✉ Commercial Street/Dock Street, Leith EH6 6EY ☎ 0131 555 1390 🚌 1, 11, 22, 34, 35, 36, Skylink 200

LEITH MARKET

stockbridgemarket.com/leith

Like its parent in Stockbridge, this farmers' market's main stocks-in-trade are locally sourced produce and innovative, multinational street snacks. It hosts a special Vegan Quarter on the first Saturday of each month. You'll also find a choice of artisan-made clothes and accessories.

➕ Off map ✉ Dock Place, Commercial Street EH6 6LU ☎ 0131 261 6181 🕐 Sat 10–4 🚌 1, 11, 22, 34, 35, 36, Skylink 200

STOCKBRIDGE MARKET

stockbridgemarket.com

On the edge of New Town, beside the Water of Leith, this Sunday food market is a great place to sample street food from all over the world or put together a picnic from stalls selling the best local (and often organic) produce. There are also artisan craft stalls of all kinds.

➕ Off map ✉ 1 Saunders Street EH3 6TQ ☎ 0131 261 6181 🕐 Sun 10–5 (check website for changes) 🚌 24, 29, 42

THOSE WERE THE DAYS

thosewerethedaysvintage.com

Those Were The Days is a venerable St. Stephen Street institution. This is the place to go for pre-loved bridal wear, a perfect little black dress from the 1950s, a 1960s mini, 1970s flares and velvet jackets and accessories to match, for both men and women. All items are expertly cleaned and restored before going on sale.

➕ Off map ✉ 26 & 28 St. Stephen Street EH3 5AL ☎ 0131 225 4400 🚌 24, 29, 42

HAGGIS

Haggis is Scotland's national dish. It comes from an ancient recipe for using up the cheapest cuts of meat, and is traditionally eaten on Burns Night, January 25. It's a sort of large mutton sausage based on the ground-up liver, lungs and heart of a sheep, mixed with oatmeal, onion and spices, and cooked up in the sheep's stomach. It can be dry, greasy or gritty, although when made properly can be delicious—a wee dram of whisky helps wash it down. These days restaurants serve their own spicy or vegan versions of the recipe, and if you want a small taster, you'll sometimes find it on the menu as a starter.

Entertainment and Nightlife

DOMINION

dominioncinema.co.uk

This old-fashioned, family-run cinema is the ideal antidote to the multiplexes in the city. View latest releases in leather Pullman seats, or indulge in the First Class service, which offers reclining sofas with complimentary wine or beer and snacks.

🔆 Off map ✉ 18 Newbattle Terrace, Morningside EH10 4RT ☎ 0131 447 4771 (box office) 🚌 11, 16, 23, 36, X15

FOOTBALL

Edinburgh's two main professional teams are Heart of Midlothian (Hearts) and Hibernian (Hibs), who play in the Scottish Premier League. They are at home on alternate Saturday afternoons Aug–May (reserve in advance).

Hearts FC 🔆 Off map ✉ Tynecastle Stadium, McLeod Street EH11 2NL ☎ 0333 043 1874; heartsfc.co.uk 🚌 1, 2, 3, 4, 25, 33, 44

Hibs FC 🔆 Off map ✉ Easter Road Stadium, 12 Albion Place EH7 5QG ☎ 0131 661 2159; hiberianfc.co.uk 🚌 1, 35

HOLYROOD DISTILLERY

holyrooddistillery.co.uk

Occupying a 180-year-old building right next to Holyrood Park, the distillery produces both single malt whisky and gin. Tours of both production lines take place daily, and there's a shop where you can purchase the fruits of their labors.

🔆 G8 ✉ 19 St. Leonard's Lane EH8 9SH ☎ 0131 285 8973 ⏰ Daily 10–5 🚌 14

LEITH DEPOT

leithdepot.com

This restaurant and bar in a former bus depot has its own 60-capacity venue and presents an eclectic array of live folk, punk and rock, DJs and theater.

🔆 Off map ✉ 138–140 Leith Walk EH6 5DT ☎ 0131 555 4738 ⏰ Mon–Wed, Sun noon–midnight, Thu–Sat noon–1am 🚌 7, 10, 11, 12, 14, 16, 22, 25, 49

MUSSELBURGH RACECOURSE

musselburgh-racecourse.co.uk

Musselburgh Racecourse, one of the best small racecourses in Britain, hosts 28 flat and jump meetings a year, including family race days.

🔆 Off map ✉ Linkfield Road, Musselburgh, East Lothian EH21 7RG ☎ 0131 665 2859 🚌 106, 113, 124

ROYAL COMMONWEALTH POOL

edinburghleisure.co.uk

Edinburgh is proud of its Olympic-size indoor swimming pool, complete with a diving pool and waterslides.

🔆 H9 ✉ 21 Dalkeith Road EH16 5BB ☎ 0131 667 7211 🚌 2, 14, 30, 33

RUGBY

(▷ 101 for Murrayfield.)

SUMMERHALL

summerhall.co.uk

This events venue and creative hub is one of Britain's largest. It hosts everything from stand-up comedy to traditional music, drama and cinema.

🔆 Off map ✉ 1 Summerhall EH9 1PL ☎ 0131 560 1580 🚌 3, 5, 7, 8, 14, 29, 30, 31, 33, 35, 37, 45, 49

GOLF

Golf is the national game and with more than 500 courses throughout the country, it's no wonder fanatics flock to the area. The closest courses can be found at Braids Hill, Craigmillar Park and Silverknowes. Visit scottishgolfcourses.com for a list of courses in the area and reservation information.

Where to Eat

CHOP CHOP (££)

chop-chop.co.uk
The all-you-can-eat feast at this
Haymarket restaurant, where *jiaozi*
dumplings, dim sum and the traditional,
savory cuisine of northeast China rule, is
one of Edinburgh's great eating bargains.
You can bring your own wine or beer,
and the Haymarket location is handy for
the Gallery of Modern Art.
🔲 B7 ✉ 248 Morrison Street EH3 8DT
☎ 0131 221 1155 🕙 Mon–Fri noon–2, 5.30–
10, Sat–Sun 12.30–2.30, 5–10 🚊 Haymarket
🚌 12, 16, 31, X17, X18, Airlink 100

FISHERS LEITH (££)

fishersrestaurants.co.uk
This zesty establishment, housed in a
17th-century watchtower, serves succu-
lent fish in its brasserie-style dining
room overlooking the Water of Leith.
🔲 Off map ✉ 1 The Shore, Leith EH6 6QW
☎ 0131 554 5666 🕙 Daily noon–late 🚌 1,
11, 22, 34, 35, 36, Skylink 200

RESTAURANT MARTIN WISHART (£££)

restaurantmartinwishart.co.uk
Michelin-starred Martin Wishart's dishes
are beautifully presented at this tiny
French restaurant on the waterfront at
Leith. Bright, modern art stands out
against the white walls and stone floors.
🔲 Off map ✉ 54 The Shore, Leith EH6 6RA
☎ 0131 553 3557 🕙 Tue–Thu noon–1.30,
7–9.30, Fri–Sat noon–1.30, 6.30–9.30 🚌 1, 11,
22, 34, 35, 36, Skylink 200

RHUBARB (£££)

prestonfield.com
The food more than matches the
opulent setting at this hotel (▷ 112).
You will need to take a taxi to get here,
but it's worth the effort.
🔲 Off map ✉ Prestonfield House, Priestfield
Road EH16 5UT ☎ 0131 225 1333
🕙 Mon–Sat noon–2, 6–10, Sun 12.30–3, 6–10

THE SHIP ON THE SHORE (£££)

theshipontheshore.co.uk
Tasty seafood options at this bistro-style
bar may include whole lemon sole
meunière with french beans and baby
heritage potatoes or ship's eggs
Benedict "Royale."
🔲 Off map ✉ 24–26 The Shore, Leith EH6
6QN ☎ 0131 555 0409 🕙 Daily 9am–10pm
🚌 1, 11, 22, 34, 35, 36, Skylink 200

STARBANK INN (££)

belhavenpubs.co.uk
Right on the Newhaven waterfront, this
inn offers traditional pub food, such as
burgers (salt beef, chicken or vegan),
fish or battered halloumi and chips, or a
selection of pies, and great views over
the Firth of Forth.
🔲 Off map ✉ 64 Laverockbank Road EH5
3BZ ☎ 0131 552 4141 🕙 Mon–Wed 11–11,
Thu 11am–midnight, Fri–Sat 11am–1am, Sun
noon–11 🚌 7, 11, 16, Skylink 200

TEUCHTERS LANDING (£££)

teuchtersbar.co.uk
This is a pretty quayside restaurant in
a former lockkeeper's cottage. Fresh,
well-prepared Scottish produce is crafted
into the fish, meat and vegan dishes
that are served in intimate booths or in
the conservatory.
🔲 Off map ✉ 1a & 1c Dock Place, Leith EH6
6LU ☎ 0131 554 7427 🕙 Daily 10.30–10
🚌 1, 11, 22, 34, 35, 36, Skylink 200

Edinburgh has a diverse range of accommodations on offer, from opulent five-star hotels to lovely, if more humble, Georgian guesthouses. Scottish hospitality is in abundance throughout the city.

Introduction

Edinburgh is one of the world's favorite city-break destinations all year round. Reserving accommodations well in advance is recommended whenever you plan to travel, and essential if visiting during Festival season or over Hogmanay.

What the Grades Mean
You may notice that displayed outside all Scottish accommodations is a blue plaque with a thistle symbol. This indicates the star rating issued by VisitScotland (the Scottish Tourist Board). Every type of accommodations is assessed annually.

En Suite
Almost all hotels and guesthouses offer en-suite bathrooms, mostly with a tub.

Apartments
Edinburgh has a growing number of establishments offering self-catering studios and apartments for short-stay visitors. These can be excellent value, especially for families. Even in the city center there are plenty of supermarkets, delis and produce markets where you can buy all you need, from organic treats to microwave ready meals.

Paying
Most hotels will ask for a deposit or full payment in advance, especially for one-night bookings. Some will not take bookings for stays of only one night. Most hotels accept credit cards, but some smaller guesthouses or B&Bs may not, so check when booking.

WHEELCHAIR ACCESS

Planning and conservation limitations mean that some guesthouses and smaller boutique hotels within historic buildings are unable to provide elevators to upper floors or fully wheelchair-accessible rooms. Visitors who need wheelchair access will, however, find a wide choice of suitable accommodations in more recently built hotels all over Edinburgh, including the Old Town and New Town.

Hotels in Edinburgh come in many guises, often in beautiful old buildings

Budget Hotels

28 YORK PLACE

28yorkplace.com

This small and friendly hotel in the heart of New Town has eight rooms, each with free WiFi, rainfall shower and bath. Deluxe and superior rooms have views across New Town, and all rooms have handmade Scottish toiletries. There's a cozy lounge bar and a choice of continental or Scottish breakfast.

E4 ⊠ 28 York Place EH1 3EP ☎ 0131 524 0110 🚌 10, 11, 12, 16, 26, 44 or tram to York Place

BONNINGTON GUEST HOUSE

thebonningtonguesthouse.com

The owners extend a warm welcome at this delightful Victorian house not far from Leith, with seven bedrooms finished to a high standard and retaining original features.

Off map ⊠ 202 Ferry Road EH6 4NW ☎ 0131 554 7610 🚌 7, 14, 21

CASTLE VIEW GUEST HOUSE

castleviewgh.com

Few independent budget hotels in Edinburgh can match this 18-room guesthouse in a New Town Georgian town house for location or value for money. It offers convenient family rooms as well as doubles and twins, but note there is no elevator.

C5 ⊠ 30 Castle Street EH2 3HT ☎ 0131 226 5784 🚌 10, 11, 12, 16, 41, 42

DENE GUEST HOUSE

deneguesthouse.com

Hospitable owners offer a comfortable stay and a good breakfast at this clean and tidy Georgian town house. The New Town location makes it ideal for visiting the main sights.

C2 ⊠ 7 Eyre Place EH3 5ES ☎ 0131 556 2700 🚌 23, 27

ELDER YORK GUEST HOUSE

elderyork.co.uk

This charming guesthouse on the upper floors of a listed Georgian building offers superb value for money. You get a wee dram on the house on arrival, and the full Scottish breakfast will set you up for the day.

E3 ⊠ 38 Elder Street EH1 3DX ☎ 0131 556 1926 🚌 10, 11, 12, 16, 26, 44 and tram

OLD WAVERLEY HOTEL

oldwaverley.co.uk

For visitors looking for an affordable, centrally located full-service hotel within easy walking distance of Waverley Station and many of Edinburgh's top attractions, the Old Waverley, right on Princes Street, is hard to beat. Some rooms have views of the Scott Monument and the Castle.

D5 ⊠ 43 Princes Street EH2 2BY ☎ 0131 556 4648 🚌 All buses to Waverley Station or tram

THE PLACE

yorkplace-edinburgh.co.uk

This boutique property offers charming contemporary luxury at rates that are within most budgets. Comfortable rooms and suites with power showers, orthopedic mattresses and luxury toiletries are complemented by a stylish cocktail lounge, restaurant and a covered terrace with a barbecue and big sports screen in summer.

E4 ⊠ 34–38 York Place EH1 3HU ☎ 0131 556 7575 🚌 10, 11, 12, 16, 26, 44 or tram to York Place

Mid-Range Hotels

12 PICARDY PLACE

picardyplace.co.uk

This chic hotel in buzzy Broughton is near York Place tram stop. The 10 bedrooms are decorated in gray and cream, and the stone-floored bathrooms have tubs and rainfall showers. The hotel has two restaurants and a bar with terrace.

🔲 F4 ⊠ 12 Picardy Place EH1 3JT ☎ 0131 556 1289 🚌 1, 4, 5, 7, 8, 14, 19, 22, 25, 45, 45, 49 or tram to York Place

21212

21212restaurant.co.uk

The fancy 21212 restaurant on the grand Royal Terrace beside Calton Hill has four elegantly designed bedrooms. Each has a lounge area and enjoys splendid views of the Royal Terrace Gardens or the city and Firth of Forth.

🔲 G4 ⊠ 3 Royal Terrace EH7 5AB ☎ 0131 523 1030 🚌 1, 5, 19, 26, 34, 44, 45

23 MAYFIELD

23mayfield.co.uk

A beautifully preserved mid-Victorian house graced with mahogany paneling and period furniture, 23 Mayfield offers a glorious taste of gracious living. Relax in comfort in the Club Room, with its comfortable Chesterfield furniture and books dating back to the 1740s.

🔲 Off map ⊠ 23 Mayfield Gardens EH9 2BX ☎ 0131 667 5806 🚌 3, 7, 8, 29, 31, 37, 47, 49, 300

ANGELS SHARE HOTEL

angelssharehotel.com

This trendy hotel in Edinburgh's West End has comfortable rooms each themed on a Scottish celebrity, from Sean Connery to Sir Chris Hoy. Close to some of Edinburgh's best shopping and nightlife, it also has its own restaurant and late-night cocktail bar.

🔲 B6 ⊠ 9–11 Hope Street EH2 4EL ☎ 0131 247 7000 🚌 41, 43, 47, 104, 113, X5, X7, X19, X37, X43, X47

THE BALLANTRAE

ballantraehotel.co.uk

This hotel, in a listed Georgian town house in New Town, has 19 spacious rooms with period detail. The honeymoon suite has a four-poster bed and the family room has a Jacuzzi. Next door, the Ballantrae Apartments offer self-catering apartments.

🔲 E4 ⊠ 8–12 York Place EH1 3EP ☎ 0131 478 4748 🚌 10, 11, 12, 16, 26, 44 or tram to York Place

DUNSTANE HOUSE

thedunstane.com

In the city's West End, close to Haymarket station, this pair of 1850s Victorian mansion houses have retained much of their architectural grandeur,

giving a country-house atmosphere. Some of the 35 bedrooms have four-poster beds.

🔲 Off map ✉ 4 West Coates, Haymarket EH12 5JQ ☎ 0131 337 6169 🚍 12, 16, 31, X17, X18, Airlink 100

HOTEL DU VIN

hotelduvin.com

This classy hotel is at the top end of this price bracket but it's worth looking for one of the good deals available. This former poorhouse and asylum makes much of exposed brickwork and original features. The 47 rooms and suites offer a high level of comfort and decoration. First-class food is served in the hallmark Du Vin bistro, which has a whisky snug for relaxation.

🔲 E7 ✉ 11 Bristo Place, 2 Forrest Road EH1 1EZ ☎ 0131 285 1479 🚍 41, 42, 67

THE INN ON THE MILE

theinnonthemile.co.uk

The Inn on the Mile is a bar-restaurant with stylish rooms and a grandstand view of the Royal Mile. Waverley Station is less than a 5-minute walk away. Rooms are chic, with perks like free mineral water, fluffy bathrobes and mini-bars. Guests may use the pool at the next-door Radisson Blu for a fee.

🔲 F6 ✉ 82 High Street EH1 1LL ☎ 0131 556 9940 🚍 3, 5, 7, 8, 14, 29, 30, 31, 33, 35, 37, 45, 49

KEW HOUSE

kewhouse.com

Forming part of a listed Victorian terrace, Kew House is spotless throughout and has six bright bedrooms and a comfortable lounge offering supper and snack options. It's located near Murrayfield Stadium and is just a 15-minute walk from the center of Edinburgh.

SELF-CATERING

If you are planning to stay outside Edinburgh and travel into the city daily, it is worth considering renting self-catering accommodations. The choice is good—you could stay in anything from an idyllic cottage to the wing of a castle. Even in Edinburgh itself, there are self-catering options available. The Edinburgh and Lothians Tourist Board (edinburgh.org) publishes full details of self-catering options in its annual accommodations guide and also provides a reservation service.

🔲 Off map ✉ 1 Kew Terrace, Murrayfield EH12 5JE ☎ 0131 313 0700 🚍 12, 16, 31, X17, X18, Airlink 100

THE RAEBURN

theraeburn.com

A former Scottish Boutique Hotel of the Year winner, this 10-bedroom hotel in a Georgian town house is within easy reach of city-center sights but is located away from the crowds in bohemian Stockbridge. Rooms are stylish, with roll-top baths and walk-in rain showers. The gastropub-style restaurant serves hearty dishes such as shin of beef and onion pie. For smokers, there's a covered outdoor terrace.

🔲 Off map ✉ 112 Raeburn Place EH4 1HG ☎ 0131 332 7000 🚍 24, 29, 42

THE ROYAL SCOTS CLUB

royalscotsclub.com

Handily located by Queen Street Gardens in New Town, this grand club feels like a country house hotel (and you don't have to be a member to stay here). Its 27 bedrooms have been designed with extreme comfort in mind.

🔲 D4 ✉ 29–31 Abercromby Place EH3 6QE ☎ 0131 525 6170 🚍 23, 27

Luxury Hotels

PRICES

Expect to pay over £150 per night for a double room in a luxury hotel.

THE BONHAM

thebonham.com

This West End hotel offers modern public rooms with mood lighting and striking art, and 49 bedrooms combining high standards of style with 21st-century technology. There is a refreshing contemporary feel throughout. Imaginative, European-influenced dinners in No. 35 at The Bonham highlight the chef's good use of local fresh produce.

➕ A6 ✉ 35 Drumsheugh Gardens EH3 7RN
☎ 0131 226 6050 🚌 19, 37, 41, 47, X37, X47

THE CHESTER RESIDENCE

chester-residence.com

In a row of Georgian town houses near Haymarket rail station, the Chester is a collection of 23 stylish serviced apartments. Luxuriously fitted out, some living quarters have grand drawing rooms while others are intimate garden-side spaces.

➕ Off map ✉ 9 Rothesay Place EH3 7SL
☎ 0131 226 2075 🚌 19, 36, 37, 41, 43, 47, 101, 113, 124, X7, X24, X37, X43, X47

FINGAL

fingal.co.uk

This humble lighthouse tender once braved the roaring oceans but has now been converted into a 23-bedroom luxury floating hotel berthed in Leith's Alexandra Dock. The result is a beguiling mixture of old-world style and contemporary super-yacht glamour.

➕ Off map ✉ Alexandra Dock, Leith EH6 7DX ☎ 0131 357 5000 🚌 11, 22, 34, 35, 36, Skylink 200

GLASSHOUSE

theglasshousehotel.co.uk

Modern glass architecture strikingly embraces the facade of former Lady Glenorchy Church as you enter this chic boutique hotel. The 65 rooms have floor-to-ceiling windows that ensure spectacular views over Calton Hill. There's also a rooftop bar and garden.

➕ F4 ✉ 2 Greenside Place EH1 3AA
☎ 0131 525 8200 🚌 1, 4, 5, 7, 8, 14, 19, 22, 25, 34, 45, 49

PRESTONFIELD HOUSE

prestonfield.com

A 17th-century baroque mansion tucked away in 8ha (20 acres) of landscaped gardens south of Holyrood Park, Prestonfield is arguably the capital's most exclusive and desirable hotel.

➕ Off map ✉ Prestfield Road EH16 5UT
☎ 0131 225 7800 🚌 2, 14, 30, 33

THE SCOTSMAN

scotsmanhotel.co.uk

The former head office of *The Scotsman* newspaper in Old Town is now a luxury hotel, with 69 traditionally decorated rooms. The North Bridge Brasserie offers fine dining and the subterranean Escape leisure club has an unusual stainless steel swimming pool.

➕ E5 ✉ 20 North Bridge EH1 1TR ☎ 0131 556 5565 🚌 3, 5, 7, 8, 29, 33, 35, 37, 45, 49

WINE HOUSE 1821

winehouse1821.co.uk

Not so much a hotel as a wine bar with rooms, this sophisticated Georgian town house has sleek modern decor. Its four bedrooms are all designed with comfort in mind and come with fantastic views.

➕ F4 ✉ 4 Picardy Place EH1 3JT ☎ 0131 557 1821 🚌 1, 4, 5, 7, 8, 14, 19, 22, 25, 34, 45, 49

Use this section to help you plan your visit to Edinburgh. We have suggested the best ways to get around the city, and have included other useful information for when you are there.

Planning Ahead

When to Go

Edinburgh lies on the eastern side of Scotland, which is cooler, windier and drier than the west. At any time of year you are likely to meet rain, but the chances are it will not last for long. Some tourist sights close in winter, but major city museums stay open year-round.

AVERAGE DAILY MAXIMUM TEMPERATURES

JAN	FEB	MAR	APR	MAY	JUN	JUL	AUG	SEP	OCT	NOV	DEC
41°F	43°F	48°F	52°F	57°F	63°F	66°F	66°F	61°F	55°F	48°F	45°F
5°C	6°C	9°C	11°C	14°C	17°C	19°C	19°C	16°C	13°C	9°C	7°C

Spring (March to May) has the best chance of clear skies and sunny days.

Summer (June to August) is unpredictable—it may be hot and sunny, but it can also be cloudy and wet. This is the time you can get *haar* (sea mist) that shrouds the city in thick mist, although this can happen at other times of the year as well.

Fall (September to November) is usually more settled and there's a good chance of fine weather, but nothing is guaranteed.

Winter (December to February) can be cold, dark, wet and dreary, but there are also sparkling clear, sunny days of frost, when the light is brilliant.

WHAT'S ON

January *Burns Night* (25 Jan): the birthday of Scotland's bard, celebrated throughout Scotland with haggis and whisky.
March/April *Edinburgh Science Festival*: science and technology events at various venues.
Ceilidh Culture: events centered around traditional Scottish arts.
May *Edinburgh International Children's Festival*: Britain's largest performing arts festival for young people.
Edinburgh Marathon.
June *Edinburgh International*

Film Festival: (▷ 41, panel).
Royal Highland Show: Scotland's biggest agricultural show.
July/August *Edinburgh Jazz & Blues Festival*: 10 days of jazz performed by big names and new talent.
August *Edinburgh International Festival*: over three weeks, some of the world's best plays, opera, music and dance.
Edinburgh Festival Fringe: A chance to see tomorrow's stars strut their stuff.
Edinburgh Military Tattoo: (▷ 5).

International Book Festival: occupies a tented village in Charlotte Square.
Mela: a vibrant celebration of cultural diversity with music, dance and street performers.
October *Scottish International Storytelling Festival*: attracts storytellers from home and abroad.
November/December *Edinburgh's Christmas*: German and Scottish Christmas markets, ice rink, Ferris wheel and more.
December/January *Edinburgh Hogmanay*: (▷ 13).

Edinburgh Online

visitscotland.com
The official VisitScotland website, with a comprehensive database of information covering everything from weather, transportation and events to shopping, nightlife and places to stay throughout Scotland.

eif.co.uk
An exhaustive guide to what's on at the Edinburgh International Festival.

edinburghguide.com
An informative guide to attractions, entertainment, recreation, eating out and accommodations, plus links to other sites.

nms.ac.uk
The National Museum of Scotland looks after many of Scotland's important museum collections. Its website provides detailed information about the museums in its care.

undiscoveredscotland.co.uk
An online guide to Scotland. The Edinburgh section has many useful links to other good sources of information.

nts.org.uk
The National Trust for Scotland looks after historic buildings in Scotland, including some in Edinburgh. Its website gives updated information about all the properties it is responsible for.

historicenvironment.scot
This website has information on more than 300 listed buildings and ancient sites safeguarded by Historic Environment Scotland.

thehotelguru.com
Nearly 50 of Edinburgh's best boutique hotels and guesthouses are reviewed and can be booked on this website, which also lists places to stay throughout Scotland and the rest of the UK.

TRAVEL SITES

fodors.com
A complete travel-planning site. You can research prices and weather; reserve air tickets, cars and rooms; pose questions to (and get answers from) fellow visitors; and find links to other sites.

visitbritain.com
Great places to visit around the UK, with accommodations, transportation, special offers and travel tips.

ONLINE ACCESS

Free WiFi access is available at many cafés and bars throughout the city center (including branches of Caffè Nero and Costa Coffee) and in almost all hotels and guesthouses. Surprisingly, some larger hotels belonging to international chains still charge extra for WiFi in bedrooms—a service that most smaller places provide free.

Getting There

● Visitors from outside the UK must have a passport, valid for at least six months from the date of entry.
● Before traveling, visitors from outside the UK should check visa requirements. See ukvisas.gov.uk or uk.usembassy.gov.

CUSTOMS

● At the time of writing, EU nationals do not have to declare goods imported for their own use (though large amounts of certain items may be questioned). This may change from 2021, once the UK has fully left the EU.
● The limits for non-EU visitors are 200 cigarettes or 50 cigars or 250g of tobacco; 1 liter of alcohol (over 22 percent alcohol) or 2 liters of wine; 50g of perfume.

BREXIT

Visitors from the EU should check the very latest entry requirements as a result of the UK's decision to leave the EU. Check if any visa or passport requirements have changed and if reduced-cost medical treatment with the European Health Insurance Card (EHIC) is still available.

AIRPORTS

There are direct flights to Edinburgh from other parts of the UK and from continental Europe. United flies direct from Chicago and Air Canada flies direct from Toronto. Several airlines fly direct from North America to Glasgow International Airport (glasgowairport.com), which is around 90 minutes from Edinburgh by road or train.

19km (12 miles)
13km (8 miles)
6.5km (4 miles)
✈ Edinburgh International Airport

FROM EDINBURGH INTERNATIONAL AIRPORT

Edinburgh International Airport (edinburgh airport.com) is 20–30 minutes from the city center by bus, tram or cab.

The tram runs between the airport and York Place, with intermediate stops at Murrayfield, Haymarket Station and along Princes Street. Airlink 100 buses operate between the airport and Waverley Bridge, in the city center, every 10 minutes around the clock (every 15 minutes between 1 and 4am) and cost £4.50 one way or £7.50 round trip. Skylink 200 buses leave from stop B, to the left as you leave the terminal building, for Ocean Terminal in Leith; the same fares apply. The N22 night bus also leaves from outside the terminal and runs from the airport to the city center and Ocean Terminal in Leith. Journey time is around 45 minutes: flat fare is £3.

The airport cab rank is opposite the Arrivals Hall, on the ground floor of the parking garage. The cab fare to the city center is £25–£30.

INTERNAL FLIGHTS

Within the UK and Ireland, you can fly to Edinburgh from Belfast, Birmingham, Cardiff, Cork, Derry, Dublin, East Midlands, Exeter, Kirkwall, London (City, Gatwick, Heathrow, Luton and Stansted), Manchester, Newquay, Norwich, Shannon, Southampton, Stornoway and Sumburgh.

ARRIVING BY RAIL

Edinburgh has two major rail stations: Edinburgh Haymarket and Edinburgh Waverley. Waverley is a main hub for travel within Scotland, and has tourist information desks and other facilities. Regular trains connect Edinburgh with England, via the West Coast Main Line or East Coast Main Line. Most internal services are run by ScotRail (scotrail.co.uk). For further details of fares and services contact the National Rail Enquiries (tel 03457 484950 or +44 20 7278 5240 from outside the UK, nationalrail.co.uk).

ARRIVING BY COACH

Coaches arrive in Edinburgh from England, Wales and all over Scotland at Edinburgh bus station. The main coach companies operating here are National Express (nationalexpress. com) and Scottish Citylink (citylink.co.uk). There is a taxi rank on North St. David Street which can be accessed from the arrivals concourse.

ARRIVING BY CAR

One-way systems, narrow streets, red routes and dedicated bus routes and a 20mph (32km/h) speed limit make driving in the historic city center difficult. Limited on-street parking is mostly pay-and-display between 8.30am and 6.30pm Mon–Sat. There are some designated parking areas, to the south of Princes Street; the biggest is at Greenside Place, off Leith Street. Gas stations are normally open Mon–Sat 6am–10pm, Sun 8am–8pm, though some (often self-service) are open 24 hours. All take credit cards.

INSURANCE

Check your insurance coverage and buy a supplementary policy if needed. EU visitors should check the latest post-Brexit rules before traveling. Full health and travel insurance is advised for all visitors.

CONSULATES

All embassies are located in London but the following consulates are based in Edinburgh:

● French Consulate ✉ West Parliament Square EH1 1RF ☎ email only: edimbourg-fslt@diplomatie. gouv.fr

● German Consulate ✉ 16 Eglinton Crescent EH12 5DG ☎ 0131 337 2323

● Irish Consulate ✉ 16 Randolph Crescent EH3 7TT ☎ 0131 226 7711

● Netherlands Consulate ✉ Baird House, 4 Lower Gilmore Bank EH3 9QP ☎ 07731 53120

● Spanish Consulate ✉ 63 North Castle Street EH2 3LJ ☎ 0131 220 1843

● US Consulate ✉ 3 Regent Terrace EH7 5BW ☎ 0131 556 8315

Getting Around

BY BUS AND TRAM

Edinburgh's city bus network (lothianbuses. com) reaches every part of the city and beyond. Services include a 24-hour Airlink 100 service (edinburghairport.com/transport-links) between Edinburgh International Airport and Waverley Bridge in the city center, with intermediate stops including Haymarket Station. In the city, a flat-fare, one-way bus or tram ride costs £1.70 for an adult (exact fare only) and 80p for children (5–11 years). Day tickets permitting 24 hours' unlimited bus and tram travel (within the central zone) cost £4 for an adult, £2 for a child and £8.50 for a family of up to five, and can be bought online from lothianbuses.com or from the Travelshop at Waverley Bridge.

You can also buy a Ridacard for unlimited travel on buses and trams for a week or four weeks, or download m-tickets to your mobile device (minimum spend £4). If you travel on several buses and/or trams on the same day and pay by contactless credit card, the total fare will automatically be capped at £4.

Find timetables and fare information online at lothianbuses.com or at Travel Hubs at Waverley Bridge (Mon–Sat 8–6, Sun 9–5) or 49 Shandwick Place EH2 4SD (Mon–Fri 8–6, Sat 9–5, Sun 10–4).

TAXIS

Licensed taxis operate a reliable day and night service. Fares are metered and strictly regulated. Cabs can be hailed on the street or found at designated ranks at the airport, Haymarket Station, Waverley Bridge (outside Waverley Station), outside St. Andrew Square coach terminus on North St. Andrew Street and outside Balmoral Hotel at the east end of Princes Street. Private hire cabs can also be booked in advance or called by phone (City Cabs 0131 228 1211; Central Radio taxis 0131 229 2468).

CAR RENTAL

The major international car rental brands have offices at the airport with direct access to the

terminal. Several have city-center outlets. Some (including Hertz and Enterprise) advertise these as being located at Waverley Station but they may be a short walk away, on or near Picardy Place at the top of Leith Walk. If you plan on renting a car, choose accommodations that offer private car parking.

BICYCLE RENTAL

Edinburgh's largest bike rental outfit is Biketrax (tel 0131 228 6633, biketrax.co.uk), which has hybrid city bikes, lightweights, electric bikes and folding bikes. Cycle Scotland (tel 0131 556 5560, cyclescotland.co.uk) rents mountain and road bikes, hybrids, electric bikes and tandems.

ORGANIZED SIGHTSEEING

A guided tour is a good way to gain more in-depth knowledge about Edinburgh. If time is short, take one of the open-top buses that wind their way around the city sights; all tours depart from Waverley Bridge and there are four types to choose from, all of which you can hop on and hop off at your leisure (tel 0131 475 0618, edinburghtour.com). A commentary is available in a number of languages.

Various companies offer coach tours in and around the city. Try Rabbie's Trail Burners (tel 0131 226 3133, rabbies.com), which runs mini-coach (16-seater) tours to destinations such as Loch Ness and St. Andrews.

For those who prefer two wheels, another option is Edinburgh Bike Tours (tel 07753 136676, edinburghbiketours.co.uk), which offers full-day and half-day guided tours with all equipment provided.

Mercat Walking Tours offers explorations of secret underground vaults, ghost walks, *Outlander* locations walks and history tours with dramatic commentaries (Mercat House, 28 Blair Street EH1 1QR, tel 0131 225 5445, mercattours.com). Sandemans runs free, 2.5-hour walking tours year round. Tours usually leave on the hour 10–2 from Frankie and Benny's, 130 High Street (neweuropetours.eu).

VISITORS WITH DISABILITIES

● Capability Scotland (✉ 1 Osborne Terrace, Edinburgh EH12 5HG ☎ 0131 337 9876; capability-scotland.org. uk) can advise on travel requirements to ensure a smooth trip.

● disabledgo.com is an internet service giving access information to people with disabilities, as well as other advice useful when visiting Edinburgh. Restaurants, cafés, shops and attractions are all covered.

● Useful information for visitors with disabilities can be found in VisitScotland's publication *Practical Information for Visitors with Disabilities*, available from the tourist board or from tourist offices.

STUDENT VISITORS

● Students can get reduced-cost entry to some museums and attractions by showing a valid student card.

● Budget accommodations are available (▷ 109).

● There are reduced fares on buses and trains for under 16s.

Essential Facts

MONEY

Scotland's currency is pounds sterling (£), in notes of £5, £10, £20, £50 and £100. Coins are issued in values of 1p, 2p, 5p, 10p, 20p, 50p, £1 and £2. England's notes are legal tender in Scotland. Three Scottish banks (Bank of Scotland, Royal Bank of Scotland and Clydesdale Bank) also issue their own sterling notes, which circulate throughout Scotland. These may not be accepted elsewhere in the UK and are hard to exchange outside the UK, so spend them (or exchange them for Bank of England notes at a bank) before leaving Scotland.

TIPPING

In upscale restaurants, a tip of 10 percent is the norm. In smaller eating places, a tip is welcomed but not mandatory. Taxi drivers, tour guides, hairdressers and bar staff (except in more expensive establishments) do not normally expect to be tipped, though a gratuity for better-than-average service will be welcome.

ELECTRICITY

● Britain is on 240 volts AC, and plugs have three square pins. If you are bringing an electrical appliance from another country where the voltage is the same, a plug adaptor will suffice. If the voltage is different, as in the US—110 volts—you need a converter.

● Small appliances such as razors can run on a 50-watt converter, while appliances that heat up, such as irons and hairdryers, require a 1,600-watt converter.

EMERGENCY TELEPHONE NUMBERS

● For Police, Ambulance, Fire call 999 or 112.

● For non-emergency police enquiries call 101.

● If you break down driving your own car, you can call the Automobile Association and join on the spot if you are not already a member (tel 0800 887766). Check if your home country membership entitles you to reciprocal assistance. If you are driving a rental car, call the emergency number in your documentation.

MEDICINES AND MEDICAL TREATMENT

● Citizens from the EU are entitled to free or reduced-cost NHS (National Health Service) treatment until the end of 2020; after that new rules may apply. Full health and travel insurance is still advised in any case.

● Those visiting from outside the EU should have full travel and health insurance.

● For medical emergencies call 999 or 112 or go to the nearest hospital accident and emergency department.

● The 24-hour emergency department is at the Royal Infirmary of Edinburgh (51 Little France Crescent, Old Dalkeith Road EH16 4SA, tel 0131 536 1000).

● For minor injuries, the Western General Hospital (Crewe Road South EH4 2XU, tel 0131 537 1000, open daily 8am–9pm) has a walk-in service. For advice from a specialist nurse, call NHS24 on 111 or see nhs24.scot.

● To find the nearest dentist, call Lothian Dental Advice Line (tel 0131 536 4800). Walk-in

dental treatment is available at Chalmers Dental
Centre (3 Chalmers Street, tel 0131 536 4800,
open Mon–Thu 9–4.45, Fri 9–4.15).

● Pharmacies and large supermarkets sell a
range of medicines over the counter but
items such as antibiotics require a prescription.

● There are no 24-hour pharmacies in
Edinburgh. Boots the Chemist (48 Shandwick
Place, tel 0131 225 6757) has the longest
opening hours (Mon–Fri 7.30am–8pm, Sat
9–6, Sun 10.30–5).

● If you are planning to spend much time in the
countryside around Edinburgh in high summer,
beware of "midgies," the Scottish relative of tiny
biters known in the US as "no-see'ums." Most
pharmacies sell a range of remedies that will
help prevent them from blighting a picnic.

● Bear in mind, too, that in high summer the
Scottish sun can burn, despite cool breezes.
Use sunblock and sunscreen, particularly on
young children.

NATIONAL HOLIDAYS
● New Year's Day (January 1)
● New Year's Holiday (January 2)
● Good Friday
● Easter Monday
● First Monday in May
● Last Monday in May
● First Monday in August
● Last Monday in August
● Christmas Day (December 25)
● Boxing Day (December 26)
● Most places of interest close on New Year's
Day, 1 May and Christmas, while others close
on all public holidays.

OPENING TIMES
● Banks: Mon–Fri 9.30–4.30; larger branches
open Sat morning.
● Post offices: Mon–Fri 9–5.30, Sat 9–12.
● Shops: most shops open daily 9–5, including
Sundays.
● Museums: opening times vary widely; see
individual entries.

PERSONAL SAFETY

● Levels of violent crime
are relatively low but there
are areas to avoid, as in
every city. At night these
include the backstreet and
dockside areas of Leith,
wynds (narrow lanes) off
the Royal Mile, the foot-
paths across the Meadows
and unlit urban areas.

● Scottish police officers
wear a peaked flat hat with
a black-and-white check
band and are friendly and
approachable.

● Petty theft is the most
common problem, so
don't carry more cash than
you need and beware of
pickpockets, especially in
the main tourist areas and
on public transportation.
Do not hang bags on backs
of chairs.

TOILETS

Public toilets are hard to
find in the city center. There
is a small charge to use
toilets at rail and bus stations. Pubs and café-bars
frown on visitors who use
their toilets without buying
a drink. Smaller cafés that
do not serve alcohol are not
required to have toilet facilities. There are free toilets
in all the museums and art
galleries and in the Central
Library and the National
Library of Scotland, both on
George IV Bridge.

NEWSPAPERS AND MAGAZINES

● Subscribe free to *The Edinburgh Reporter* (theedinburghreporter. co.uk) for twice-daily online reports of events, sports fixtures, new restaurant and bar openings and more.
● *The Leither* (free in the best bars from Leith to Broughton and Stockbridge) speaks its own distinctive voice about local events and global issues.
● *The Skinny* (theskinny. co.uk) offers "independent cultural journalism" to a mainly student audience looking for great nights out.

TELEPHONE SERVICES

● Various companies offer directory enquiry services. The British Telecom numbers are:
● Directory Enquiries ☎ 118 500 (77p per call plus £1.55 per minute)
● International Directory Enquiries ☎ 118 505 (£2.50 per call plus 75p per minute)
● International Operator ☎ 155
● Operator ☎ 100

POST OFFICES

● The main post office is at St. James Centre, St. Andrew Square. It's open Mon–Sat 9–5.30. Most other post offices are open on weekdays and Saturday mornings.
● Many newspaper shops and supermarkets sell stamps.
● Postboxes are painted red; collection times are shown on each box.

RADIO AND TELEVISION

● Scotland is served by UK national radio stations, and most Scottish regions and cities also have their own stations. Edinburgh's Radio Forth (97.3FM) broadcasts a mix of news, music, traffic reports and weather forecasts.
● BBC Radio Scotland (92.5–94.7FM) broadcasts a similar mix but covers the whole of Scotland.
● Digital and satellite TV stations available in Scotland include all BBC national channels, ITV, STV, CNN and Sky channels.

TELEPHONES AND WIFI

● The code for Edinburgh is 0131. Omit this when making a local call.
● Payphones can be found at the airport, coach station, railway stations and elsewhere in the city center. They may accept coins, but more usually credit and debit cards. BT (British Telecom) payphones cost a minimum of 60p for cash payments and £1.20 for card; the minimum charge includes a 40p connection charge and two calling time units of 10p.
● Mobile phone coverage is good but not all US and Canadian cell phones will work in the UK, and roaming charges may be very high.
● To call the US from Scotland dial 00 1, followed by the number. To call Scotland from the US, dial 011 44, then the customer's number without the initial 0.
● Free wireless internet is provided throughout the city center by City of Edinburgh's EdiFree WiFi system. Find a map of WiFi hotspots at edinburghfreewifi.com.

Language

Standard English is the official language of Scotland, and is spoken everywhere. However, as with other parts of Britain, the Scottish people have their own variations on the language and the way it is spoken. You should have no difficulty understanding the people of Edinburgh, who tend automatically to moderate their accent when speaking to non-Scots. But many Scottish words and phrases are used in everyday conversation.

COMMON WORDS AND PHRASES

auld	old	*een*	eyes
awfy	very	*fash*	bother
aye/naw	yes/no	*gae*	go
belong	come from	*glen*	valley
ben	hill, mountain	*gloaming*	dusk
bide	live	*guttered*	drunk
birle	spin, turn	*haar*	sea mist
blether	to chatter, gossip	*haver*	talk nonsense
		Hogmanay	New Year's Eve
bonnie	pretty, attractive	*ken*	to know
braw	fine, good	*kirk*	church
burn	stream	*lassie*	girl
canny	cunning, clever	*lum*	chimney
ceilidh	party or dance	*messages*	shopping
couthy	comfortable	*nicht*	night
dinnae	don't	*och*	oh
douce	gentle and kind	*Sassenach*	English person
dram	a measure of whisky	*trews*	tartan trousers
		wee	small

SCOTTISH DIALECT IN LITERATURE

Robert (or "Rabbie") Burns (1759–96) is Scotland's best-loved poet. He wrote his verse either in the Scots tongue or in an English that he flavored with Scots dialect words. This opening stanza from his famous poem "To a Mouse" (1786) is a fine example of his mastery of the form:

Wee, sleekit cow'rin', tim'rous beastie,
O what a panic's in thy breastie!
Thou need na start awa sae hasty,
Wi' bickering brattle!
I wad be laith to rin an' chase thee,
Wi' murd'ring pattle!

Timeline

EARLY SETTLERS

The area was first settled by hunting tribes around 3000BC and in about 1000BC the first farmers were joined by immigrant Beaker People, who introduced pottery and metalworking skills. Parts of Scotland were held by the Romans for a short time. After their departure in the 5th century AD the area suffered waves of invasion.

THE MACALPINS

Northumbrians held southern Scotland for 33 years, but were defeated in 1018 by MacAlpin king Malcolm II. Malcolm III married Margaret, sister of Edgar Atheling, heir to the English throne, but was usurped by William the Conqueror.

From left to right: Robert the Bruce statue; James VI of Scotland; the Forth Rail Bridge; posters for the Edinburgh Festival; Holyrood Park hosts Fringe Festival events

6th century AD The Gododdin, a Celtic tribe, make their seat at Dun Eidinn.

638 Dun Eidinn falls to the Angles of Northumbria and is renamed Edinburgh.

1018 Edinburgh and Lothian conquered by Malcolm II.

1110 David I builds St. Margaret's Chapel.

1128 Foundation of Holyrood Abbey.

1296–1357 Scottish Wars of Independence. Castle alternates between English and Scottish control but Scotland retains independence.

1437 Edinburgh becomes royal capital.

1501 James I begins Palace of Holyroodhouse.

1544 English forces sack Edinburgh but fail to take Castle.

1603 James VI succeeds to English throne as James I, thus uniting the Scottish and English crowns, and moves court to London.

1707 Scottish Parliament ratifies the Act of Union and Edinburgh ceases to be Scotland's seat of government.

1767 Construction of New Town begins.

1776 North Bridge completed. Royal Observatory opens on Calton Hill.

1822 George IV is the first British monarch to visit Edinburgh since Charles II in 1651.

1847 North British Railway advertises first Edinburgh–London service.

1890 Forth Bridge carries first trains between Edinburgh and northern Scotland.

1947 First Edinburgh International Festival held.

1964 Forth Road Bridge opens.

1997 Scots vote for devolution, allowing for a Scottish Parliament within the UK.

1999 The Scottish Parliament sits for the first time since 1707.

2004 Scottish Parliament moves into new building at Holyrood.

2014 Referendum on Scottish independence results in a "no" vote.

2017 Opening of Queensferry Crossing, a major new road bridge next to the historic Forth Bridges.

2020 Seventieth anniversary of the Royal Military Tattoo.

EDINBURGH'S FAMOUS

Some of Edinburgh's most famous citizens have had a significant impact on our lives. Alexander Graham Bell invented the telephone in 1847, and anesthetics were pioneered by James Young Simpson. John Knox reformed Scotland's religion and architect Robert Adam and artists Henry Raeburn and Allan Ramsay brought their flair to the buildings of the city. The literary impact has been phenomenal, through the romances of Sir Walter Scott, who was born in the city in 1771, and the detective stories of Sir Arthur Conan Doyle. More fame comes from Robert Louis Stevenson, author of *Kidnapped* and *Treasure Island*, who was born here in 1850, and actor Sean Connery, who spent his early days here.

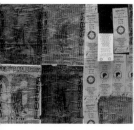

Index

Edinburgh 25 Best

WRITTEN BY Hilary Weston, Jackie Staddon and Sally Roy
UPDATED BY Dixe Wills
SERIES EDITOR Clare Ashton
COVER DESIGN Jessica Gonzalez
DESIGN WORK Liz Baldin
IMAGE RETOUCHING AND REPRO Ian Little

ISBN 978-1-64097-336-7

FIFTH EDITION

Printed and bound in China by 1010 Printing Group Limited.

10 9 8 7 6 5 4 3 2 1

A05743
Contains Ordnance Survey data © Crown copyright and database right 2020
Transport map © Communicarta Ltd, UK

We would like to thank the following photographers, companies and picture libraries for their assistance in the preparation of this book:

All images are copyright AA/K Paterson except:

2–18t AA/E Ellington; 4tl AA/K Blackwell; 5 Jonathan Cohen/Alamy Stock Photo; 6c AA/M Taylor; 6cr AA/J Smith; 6bl AA/J Smith; 6bcl AA/J Smith; 6br AA/J Smith; 7tl AA/J Smith; 7tr Edinburgh Inspiring Capital; 10ctr Edinburgh Inspiring Capital; 10cr Edinburgh Inspiring Capital; 10/11b Those Were The Days Vintage Fashion & Bridal Boutiques; 11ctl AA/S Whitehorne; 11cl Edinburgh Inspiring Capital; 13 (i) AA; 13 (ii) Edinburgh Inspiring Capital; 13 (iii) Edinburgh Inspiring Capital; 13 (iv) Ian Georgeson/Alamy Stock Photo; 14br AA/I Love; 16br Hendersons of Edinburgh; 17tcl Edinburgh Inspiring Capital; 17cl The Bonham Hotel; 17bl The Glasshouse Hotel; 18tr Edinburgh Inspiring Capital; 18tcr Edinburgh Inspiring Capital; 18cr Edinburgh Inspiring Capital; 18br Brand X Pics; 19b VisitScotland/ Kenny Lam; 20 © Crown Copyright HES; 24l AA/J Smith; 24r AA/J Smith; 24/25 AA/J Smith; 25t Edinburgh Inspiring Capital; 25c AA/J Smith; 25cr AA/J Smith; 26l AA/D Corrance; 27l Edinburgh Inspiring Capital; 27r Copyright National Museums of Scotland(1); 28tl AA/S Whitehorne; 28tr AA/S Whitehorne; 28cl AA/J Smith; 29 John Peter Photography/Alamy Stock Photo; 30l AA/J Smith; 30r AA/J Smith; 31 The Scotch Whisky Experience; 32–35t AA/J Smith; 32bl AA/J Smith; 32br AA/S Whitehorne; 33bl AA/J Smith; 34br The Real Mary King's Close; 34 © The Trustees of the National Museums of Scotland; 35bl Eye Ubiquitous/Alamy Stock Photo; 37 AA/S Whitehorne; 38/39t Edinburgh Inspiring Capital; 40/41t AA/J Smith; 42–44t Edinburgh Inspiring Capital; 45 Adam Elder/Scottish Parliament; 49 Iain Masterton/ Alamy Stock Photo; 50 AA/J Smith; 50/51t Douglas Robertson; 50/51c AA/J Smith; 51 Douglas Robertson; 52l Our Dynamic Earth; 52r Our Dynamic Earth; 53l AA/J Smith; 54r FocusEurope/Alamy Stock Photo; 56l AA/D Corrance; 56r AA/J Smith; 56/7 AA/R Elliot; 57t AA/J Smith; 58l Edinburgh Inspiring Capital; 58r Adam Elder/ Scottish Parliament; 59 Andrew Cowan/Scottish Parliament; 60t AA/D Corrance; 60bl AA/J Smith; 60bl AA/J Smith; 60br AA/J Smith; 61t Adam Elder/Scottish Parliament; 62 Steve Vidler/Alamy Stock Photo; 63 Adam Goodwin/Alamy Stock Photo; 64t Edinburgh Inspiring Capital; 64c AA; 65 Iain Masterton/Alamy Stock Photo; 68l AA/R Elliot; 70 AA/I Love; 70/71t AA/K Blackwell; 72l National Gallery of Scotland; 73cl National Gallery of Scotland; 73cr National Gallery of Scotland; 74l Adam Goodwin/Alamy Stock Photo; 74r AA/J Smith; 75b Stuart Robertson/ Alamy Stock Photo; 76b © National Galleries of Scotland; 77 AA/J Smith; 81 Edinburgh Inspiring Capital; 82-3t Edinburgh Inspiring Capital; 83c The Glasshouse Hotel; 84–86t The Glasshouse Hotel; 90 © Crown Copyright HES; 90/1 © Crown Copyright HES; 92t Monica Wells/Alamy Stock Photo; 93cr AA/K Blackwell; 94l I Love; 96r RZSS Edinburgh Zoo; 97t RZSS Edinburgh Zoo; 97cl RZSS Edinburgh Zoo; 97cr RZSS Edinburgh Zoo; 100b Photo Allan Pollok Morris, Courtesy of Jupiter Artland; 102t AA/R Elliot; 102bl AA/J Smith; 102br AA/J Smith; 103 AA/J Smith; 105 AA/J Smith; 106 Imagestate; 108–112t AA/C Sawyer; 108 (i) Edinburgh Inspiring Capital; 108 (iii) AA/D Corrance; 108 (iv) Edinburgh Inspiring Capital; 114–125t Edinburgh Inspiring Capital; 124bl AA/J Smith; 124bc AA; 124br AA/J Smith.

Every effort has been made to trace the copyright holders, and we apologize in advance for any accidental errors. We would be happy to apply the corrections in the following edition of this publication.

Titles in the Series

- Amsterdam
- Bangkok
- Barcelona
- Berlin
- Boston
- Brussels and Bruges
- Budapest
- Chicago
- Dubai
- Dublin
- Edinburgh
- Florence
- Hong Kong
- Istanbul
- Krakow
- Las Vegas
- Lisbon
- London
- Madrid
- Melbourne
- Milan
- Montréal
- Munich
- New York City
- Orlando
- Paris
- Rome
- San Francisco
- Seattle
- Shanghai
- Singapore
- Sydney
- Tokyo
- Toronto
- Venice
- Vienna
- Washington, D.C.